But I Love Him

A true story of love, pain, and domestic violence

By Michelle Jewsbury

But I Love Him

A true story of love, pain, and domestic violence

By Michelle Jewsbury

Published through:
Amazon/ KDP Select

ISBN: 9781790542437
Imprint: Independently published

Editor: Jim Martyka
Cover design: Ruben Esparza Design
Front Photography: Shane McKenzie
Back Photography: Daniel Kavanaugh and Kobe Levi

First printing: 2019
Printed in the United States of America

For Daddy

I wish I would have told you. I wish I could have spent more time with you before you left this earth. You were my inspiration to work hard and to love unyielding, by pushing forward and never giving up. I love you and miss you with every fiber of my soul.

"What screws us up the most in life is the picture in our head of what it's supposed to be."

—Socrates

Table of Contents

Foreword

There are many misconceptions about domestic violence. In the United States, the courts continued to uphold a man's right to punish his wife with physical violence until 1871. In 1910, the U.S. Supreme Court ruled that a wife had no cause for action on an assault and battery charge against her husband because it would allow one spouse to bring accusations against the other in the courts. It wasn't until the 1970s, with the beginning of the Women's Liberation Movement, that shelters began to proliferate in the United States.

Domestic violence is considered a worldwide epidemic. It does not discriminate nor differentiate based on race, occupation, economic status, citizenship, religion, or even gender. *But I Love Him* is an exceptional, honest, and brave personal recollection of overcoming the destructive cycle of domestic violence. Michelle shares her story with transparency and courage. She speaks to people all over the world, explaining the mass misunderstanding and denial surrounding this pandemic.

Emotional manipulation is extremely difficult to disengage from, and Michelle has been successful in displaying the determination it takes to extricate, to survive, and ultimately thrive. At the beginning of the relationship Michelle saw warning signs, yet she chose to continue seeing him. These early risk factors included his push for quick involvement, jealousy, unrealistic expectations, isolation, blaming others for problems, sudden mood swings, and threats of violence. According to the *National Network to End Domestic Violence,* these are all red flags.

Once involved, she felt there were no other options, there was no way out. She truly believed her abuser's apologies and justifications. Like many victims, Michelle focused on what her abuser said instead of what her abuser did.

The Department of Justice states that about 61 percent of domestic violence offenders have problems with alcohol or drug abuse. As for the victims, about 20 percent of them were reported to be habitual drug users or binge drinkers themselves, and about 30 percent were drinking on the day of the assault. In Michelle's case, her abuser was physically violent while he was intoxicated. Michelle learned that in order to avoid physical altercations, she could track her abuser's alcohol consumption but as you read you will discover it didn't always work. The emotional abuse Michelle suffered was constant. Her abuser excelled in manipulation and exploitation.

As recently as 1977, the California Penal Code stated that wives charging husbands with criminal assault and battery must suffer more injuries than commonly needed for charges of battery. Emotional abuse isn't seen on the outside. When children are young, they are taught that "sticks and stones will break your bones but words will never hurt you." What you learned when you were young is incorrect. Emotional abuse hurts just as physical abuse does. They are just different kinds of pain.

One in four women and one in seven men will experience domestic violence in their lifetime. Finally, in 1984, the Family Violence Prevention and Services Act was passed in an effort to prevent more incidents of family violence and to provide shelter to those victimized. There is much that still needs to be done before eradicating this global catastrophe.

According to the *Childhood Domestic Violence Association*, children who witness domestic violence are fifteen times more likely to be victims of child abuse. Even witnessing violence is painful and overwhelming. Kids believe they are to blame for the violence. Being around violence or being the target of violence leaves people, both adults and children alike, with difficulties in functioning emotionally, physically, and socially. Children growing up in a violent domestic situation are 74 percent more likely to commit a violent crime against someone else, thus perpetuating the cycle. The United States has one of the worst records among advanced nations, losing between four to seven children every day to neglect and/or abuse.

Michelle was diagnosed with PTSD and Battered Women's Syndrome. She has since used the telling of her story for her own recovery and for impacting thousands of people worldwide. This book sheds light on the horrors of domestic violence and its impact, but also on the path of recovery and hope and turning the lemons of her life into lemonade. This book is a mandatory read and it is with great pleasure that I introduce you to Michelle Jewsbury and her story.

Douglas L. Gosney, Psy.D., LMFT, SEP
www.TheGosneyGroup.com

Author's Note

To write this book, I relied upon my personal journals, researched facts, consulted with several of the people who appear, and tapped into the many strong and lingering memories of these events and this time in my life. I have changed the names of most but not all of the individuals in this book, and in some cases I modified identifying details in order to preserve anonymity. There are no mythological characters or events in this book. I occasionally omitted people and events, but only when that omission had no impact on either the accuracy or the substance of the story.

Introduction

As I repositioned myself on top of an overpriced, white, goose down comforter in a swanky hotel room, coughing up blood, I thought to myself that I wanted to die. How on earth did I allow myself to get into this situation...again? How was he able to convince me that the former beating was a misunderstanding, an error in judgement, that he had changed and he would never hurt me again? All the promises and the "I love you's" did not prepare me for the brutality of this beating. How did I love someone who physically and emotionally abused me? How did I love someone who got triggered by the smallest infraction, then transformed into a ferocious, violent monster with the capability to kill me? These are questions many domestic violence survivors have often asked themselves.

I laid on the bed stoic, dazed, and without movement in one of the most expensive hotel rooms on the Sunset Strip in Hollywood. I watched what my Prince Charming was going to do next to me; a mere blow to the face, a violent assault, or strangulation. I anticipated more strikes. Anything I said or any movement I made infuriated him. I was naked, bare, and unprotected. He wouldn't let me get dressed. He figured that if I could get to the door before he reached me, I wouldn't run because I had no clothes on. He came at me again. I tried to breathe while feeling the constrictive force of his strong, masculine hands around my throat. I hurt. My body hurt. I just wanted him to stop. "All I want to do is talk," he said, but every time I tried to mutter a word, the onslaught would continue.

Paul's favorite tactic was to put his left hand around my throat, squeeze to constrict air flow, and force his fingers of his right hand into my mouth pressing so vigorously under my tongue that streams of blood would pour from my wounds. I think he relished in having control over whether I lived or died. He was relentless in his assault and toyed with me. He decided if I was allowed to breathe after a few seconds or a solid minute. He decided if I could take another breath. His temper blazed with fury, his eyes the color of a black opal, and he possessed extreme strength fueled by adrenaline in his touch.

His frenzy began shortly after arriving back in our hotel room from a Dodgers game. We had a few drinks at the night club on the first floor of the hotel before we stumbled upstairs. Both of us were intoxicated from the constant flow of alcohol, we didn't go ten minutes without a drink in our hands. Paul helped me choose an outfit to wear that consisted of skin tight blue pants, a white blouse and matching high heels. I looked good. When Paul was getting drinks, I was getting attention from other men. I was propositioned with every pickup line in the book. Paul was jealous and possessive. He unraveled at the thought of me with another person. When we arrived back to our room he was fearless in showing his dominance.

He vigorously started kissing me, his hand moving downward, unzipping my pants and pulling them to the floor. He pushed me forcefully up against the wall as he passionately caressed my clitoris, locking his lips with mine, prepping me for angry, erotic, and lustful sex. I felt wanted and needed.

I made a comment about the abundance of men that advanced in my direction that evening. His appetite abruptly changed and his desire diminished. He said, "I'm tired and want to go to bed." He stopped his sexual aggression and left me standing in the entryway alone. I was confused. I followed him to the bed to make sure he was alright. "Paul what's wrong? Did I do something?" He assured me everything was fine and that he just wanted to go to sleep. I obliged, kissed him on the forehead, and went into the bathroom to take a shower.

I finished taking off my clothes, and once I started running the water, Paul unexpectedly appeared. He was furious. He picked up a knick-knack from the counter top and threw it against the wall by my head. The figurine burst into a million little pieces; that's when I knew I was in trouble. I tried to question him about what made him so upset, about what I did wrong.

"You are a slut, you don't appreciate me for all I do for you!" Paul said. "You take pleasure in other men's attention." His commentary continued with delusional and hysterical accusations.

He stumbled forward, took me by my throat, and slammed me against the drywall with so much strength that my head bounced. I kept apologizing to him through my sobs, in the hopes I would appease his devilish temper, but it didn't work. He led me out of the bathroom and threw me on the bed. He strangled me, turned me around and pressed my face forcefully on the beautiful white down comforter. The screams from my mouth were involuntary at first. I knew from previous attacks that any noise I made would result in a more severe "punishment."

Paul placed me on all fours on the bed. I was nude, defenseless and powerless. He forced me to stay on my hands and knees while he ripped his belt out of the loops of his favorite pair of 7 For All Mankind jeans. He thrust his fingers inside of me while I pleaded with him to stop.

"Is this how you like it? Hard and animalistic?" he said while penetrating me. That was when I screamed on purpose. I hoped that someone in the hotel would hear my cries.

Paul and I stayed at very lucrative establishments, ones that cost upwards of a thousand dollars per night. My experience with such properties is they respect your privacy, understanding that what happens in the hotel stays at the hotel, what they don't know won't hurt them. They also tend to turn a blind eye to domestic altercations. No one heard me that night because no one chose to listen. There were people partying in the downstairs nightclub; my whaling was competing with the music and the loud bass. I lost and the music won.

Paul kept me locked in that hotel room all night. I endured a beating and rape that lasted roughly four hours. I screamed and screamed and screamed. Every time I cried out, it made the situation worse. If I was making too much noise during his brutal attack, he would advance toward me with more determination. He would strangle me harder, with more passion and aggression. There were many times where I screamed so loud that I thought someone would come running. I wanted to get the attention of someone, anyone in the hotel to save me from the violence. No one ever came. No one saved me that night.

Due to my experience in a domestic violence relationship, my curiosity propelled me to do research. According to the *Merriam-Webster Dictionary*, domestic violence is "the inflicting of physical injury by one family or household member on another; also: a repeated or habitual pattern of such behavior."

Domestic violence is not limited to only the physical battering of a person. As cited in *The Domestic Violence Sourcebook*, psychologist and author Susan Forward has described abuse as "any behavior that is interceded to control and subjugate another human being through the use of fear, humiliation and verbal or physical assaults…it is the systematic persecution of one partner by another." Many experts believe that emotional abuse may have longer lasting implications than that of physical abuse. Many abusers use intimidation, looks, gestures and loud voices to dominate their partner.

Many researchers agree that domestic violence is not strictly a lower class problem. Affluent women suffer from violence from their spouse as well. Domestic violence occurs amongst a variety of religions, ethnic backgrounds, economic and social standings, and sexual preferences. Domestic violence covers a wide array of violence between people including spousal battery, sibling violence, violence against children and children against parents. The equally complex issues of violence amongst groups or individuals outside of spousal battering involve different dynamics that are beyond the scope of this book. There are instances where women are the abuser and men are the victims. However, most domestic violence is committed by men against women.

According to the Department of Justice, "women are victims of domestic violence eleven times more often than men." Some suggest that most violence against men often occurs while a woman is defending herself. I am not discrediting or invalidating the thousands of men, LGBTQIA individuals or children who fall prey to domestic violence. Violence of any kind against any victim is heinous.

This is my story.

I am sharing this heartbreaking time in my life so I can give people hope and confidence beyond their circumstances. I feel that my story can shed light to the thousands of individuals who do not understand domestic violence, abuse or why victims stay. I have been asked multiple times why I put up with the violence for so long. My reply is a complicated and mangled answer, an elaborate explanation to a complex issue.

I want to assist men and women who find themselves trapped in a situation similar to my own. I want these individuals to know that they are not alone. Their desire to stay with an abusive partner does not make them wrong or cowardly; it just makes them human. I want to help victims understand they are being manipulated, emotionally and psychologically tormented, and need to find a way out. You need to find a way to stay alive. I stayed because I cared, because I believed the lies, because I trusted he would change, and because I loved him. I thank God I am alive to tell my story today.

Chapter One: Growing Up

When I was a young girl, I would daydream about my Prince Charming. I would imagine that he would come whisk me off my feet atop a beautiful white stallion and save me from the normalcy of my life. I imagined that he would be like Snow White's prince who kissed her, causing her to wake from her stupor. Or make me sing like Princess Aurora from the 1959 rendition of *Sleeping Beauty.*

"I know you, I walked with you once upon a dream. I know you, the gleam in your eyes is so familiar a gleam. Yet I know it's true, that visions are seldom all they seem... but if I know you, I know what you'll do: you'll love me at once, the way you did once upon a dream..."

Love was a fairy tale to me. Real life wasn't a fairy tale however, and I had to learn that the hard way.

I was born August 1983 to two loving, hard-working parents. My dad, Bill, was a looker. He was 6'1" with blue eyes and shaggy blond hair. He met my mom, Wendy, in high school and asked her to marry him many times before she finally said yes. Her excuse was, "I'm not ready, maybe another time." She was beautiful and captivating. She had blue eyes and a mesmerizing smile. Mom eventually said yes and they were married on April 24, 1981.

My father just started his career with the U.S. Army and my mother worked as a waitress to supplement their income. Two years after they had me, my brother, Josh, came into the picture. Josh was bald and chubby. I didn't understand why he was now part of our three-person family. I was extremely jealous of him. I wanted to keep all the attention from my mom and dad and not share it with a brand new infant. I would push him off the couch and hit him over the head with a plastic baseball bat. I remember one night, my mother just finished stoking the fire and set the black iron poker in its proper place by the stove. I waited until

Mom wasn't looking and grabbed the hot stick. I walked over to Josh and pushed the hot end of the hearth tool onto his left cheek. My brother screamed, naturally. "Why sis?" he said, with tears streaming down his face. I branded him like I was a cattle owner branding my herd. I wanted my parents to be all mine and I didn't want to share. I eventually understood that I could not "get rid" of my brother so I learned to love him despite my jealousy. Every time I see Josh, I am reminded of this incident by the scar that remains on his face.

Mom and Dad were nurturing, patient parents, but they also were very young. They had me when they were only twenty-three years old. They were just beginning adulthood and still playing like they were teenagers. Dad worked during the day and partied at night. Mom joined him after her night shifts and they stayed up late into the evening with friends.

In 1990, my father joined the military full time. He went to boot camp for nine weeks in October when the autumn leaves began turning orange and red. Before his training began, an incident happened with my mom. Mom's friend Suzette framed her for possession of cocaine with intent to sell. Suzette made some kind of deal with the DA in exchange for no jail time after she was caught snorting blow. Suzette was desperate and essentially turned on one of her closest friends…my mother. She planted the drugs on the top shelf in my mom's coat closet. When the cops stormed in, they knew exactly where to look. Mom was indicted that day.

I remember that not too long after my dad left for boot camp, Mom dropped my brother and I off at school and said, "I love you both so much," with tears in her eyes. She kissed us and told us that she would pick us up once school let out. While my brother and I were in class, Mom went in for sentencing. I remember playing on the jungle gym after school with Josh, waiting for Mom to come pick us up, but she never came. We were picked up by my mom's stepparents and then quickly transferred to my dad's parents, who drove us to their home in Salt Lake City.

My dad and mom concocted a plan to get Josh and me out of town before the state could try to take us away. They didn't tell us beforehand what was going to happen; it just happened. Mom would serve her sentence and my dad would remain in boot camp to gather us later. My brother and I were scared and confused. We missed our parents and we didn't understand the arrangement. My brother was five and I was seven.

I didn't comprehend the severity of the situation or why I couldn't see my mom. Grandma said, "Your mother is in a lot of trouble, Michelle." I thought maybe I had done something wrong, that it was my fault mom was gone. I was super upset. I thought we had to stay with my grandparents because we were bad children.

My dad was in boot camp somewhere down south running in hot weather, being screamed at by his commanding officers. He was braving the strength it takes to make it through his military training and couldn't visit or call often. In the early 1990s, jails didn't allow for constant phone privileges so we hardly spoke to Mom. Josh and I barely talked to our parents for the duration of our stay.

I don't really remember much at my grandparents' house, except the day before Christmas break. I recall sitting by the huge window in the entry way watching kids walk to school in the middle of a snow storm. The blizzard was so bad that buses weren't running and my grandparents didn't want to risk our safety by driving us in the middle of ice, snow, and sleet. Grandma said, "It's just too dangerous to go to school today, Michelle." I was depressed because I had made my parents ornaments for Christmas and this was the last day I could get them before Christmas break. Dad planned to visit during Christmas and I wanted to give him a special gift. I wanted him to know that we were good kids and we wanted to come home. I cried, I screamed, and I just didn't get it.

When my dad arrived, my brother and I wouldn't leave him alone. There were pictures taken of Josh and me holding onto him like a child holding onto their favorite blanket. When he left to go back to basic training, my brother and I were devastated. I began suffering from abandonment issues.

Josh and I stayed there roughly four months before my mom was released from jail. It was late February. She said, "I drove throughout the night in a snow storm to reach you both. I missed you so much." She was hysterical and apologetic, holding us with all her might. Once reunited with my mom, we packed up our things and moved to Vermont to join Dad, who had accepted a post in Burlington, Vermont once he finished boot camp.

I frequently had nightmares after we moved. Mom would have to cover the window in my bedroom with a sleeping bag to keep the light from shining through. I rarely slept without the room being completely dark. If she didn't do that, I would lay in bed with the blankets up to my chin, scared because I saw little men with knives in the window. Eventually, the nightmares disappeared.

Once enrolled in school, Josh and I managed to teach ourselves to make friends quickly in order to survive. We understood that friends didn't last forever and people could easily be taken away from us. I think this is where I started to put up a wall. I was terrified to be left alone for any extended period of time. I was fearful my mom would disappear or my brother and I would be forcibly removed from our home. My imagination ran wild with delusions. I would try to be a "good girl" and began to excel in school to receive accolades from my parents, to ensure I would never be left behind again.

According to the book *Childhood Disrupted,* a study has shown a clear scientific link between adult onset of physical disease and health disorders resulting from emotional neglect and parents addicted to drugs or alcohol. This study concluded that Adverse Childhood Experiences (ACE's) pre-dispose children to adult disease. So much of what we experience as adults are inextricably linked to our childhood experiences.

Sixty-four percent of Americans have experienced something that "went wrong" in their childhood. Some 133 million Americans suffer from chronic illness while 116 million are burdened with chronic pain. Parental stress translates to children's emotional pain. Childhood experiences, both positive and negative, have a huge impact on future violence victimization. Only one third of families don't have ACE's.

Our family lived in a middle class home, went to public school, and played sports. When I was in fourth grade, we moved back to the Northwest because my dad got stationed at a local recruiting office. The impact of our first relocation from Sandpoint, Idaho to Salt Lake City left my brother and I fearful of moving. Our family relocated five times during my adolescence. My dad accepted posts in Vermont, Washington, and Hawaii. My brother and I grew familiar with switching schools and changing friends often. Dad and Mom tried to make the transition easy, but it was tough.

Christmas was the best time of year for us. My mom loved going shopping and having a ton of presents under the tree to open. Josh and I received new clothes, new shoes, and backpacks for the school year. My parents weren't religious at all and we never went to church or talked about the Bible, but I knew Christmas was Jesus' birthday, even though I had no idea who or what Jesus was.

One year, during Christmas, I asked my mom about boys. "How do you know if a boy likes you?" Mom laughed and replied, "You'll know when it happens, Michelle." I was ten years old.

I was specifically referring to a boy named Steve. We met at the local skating rink in town. I remember sitting at the edge of the floor with six other girls while we watched Steve go round and round, all of us giggling when he skated by. I fell in lust with this blue-eyed, brown-haired boy who made all the girls swoon. School wasn't where my focus was. I was more excited to go to the skating rink three times a week to see Steve. "Mom, can you drop Josh and me off before work today?" I asked. Mom obliged, and my brother and I pretty much lived at Skate Plaza Roller Rink.

Steve and I became close friends just in time for my family to move again. After I finished elementary school, my dad had to choose between moving to Seattle or Hawaii. Our family chose Hawaii. Steve and I stayed friends and whenever I could visit, I did. I was a straight-A student, but hated school. In Hawaii, I got into fights with anyone who looked at me the wrong way. Kids would taunt me. "Look at this little haole girl." I tried to ignore their comments and I learned to suppress my feelings. This was an unconscious choice. I wasn't aware that being jolted out of school, torn from my mom and dad at an early age, moving frequently, and not creating real bonds were so painful. I became numb to my childhood experiences.

I became dissociated from my feelings. *Childhood Disrupted* also states that when children are bullied, they acquire diseases and health problems as adults. One in four kids experience bullying between sixth and tenth grade.

In order to fit in, my brother participated in events for skateboarding and I became a gymnast and cheerleader. Neither one of us were popular in school. I was the "alternative cheerleader" and my brother was the kid who knew how to get into trouble.

I didn't have to work hard academically in school because it came easily for me. I wasn't being challenged and I was trying to fit in to the social norm. I was bored and began using drugs and alcohol. At thirteen years old, I started smoking marijuana. Everyone has childhood wounds and this was how I started to cope with the constant changes in my life. Drugs and alcohol were numbing tactics so I didn't have to feel pain.

My family and I stayed in Hawaii for four years. During this time, my brother and I experimented with marijuana, alcohol, mushrooms, and ecstasy. My brother's addition to this list was acid. I never tried acid but came very close on a few occasions. Josh and I snuck out of the house a number of times to go to parties or raves. I remember getting so drunk one night at a party surrounded by twenty or so people who were all older than me and passing out under a park bench. I'm lucky I wasn't sexually assaulted. On the surface, I looked fine, but underneath, I was a mess.

My mother had her own demons to deal with, stemming from what she endured in her childhood. My mom had a friend named April when she was little. Mom would go over to April's house every day after school while her mother worked. She told me that when she stayed the night at April's house, "April's dad used to make me sleep in his room on a twin size bed next to his bed. When April went to sleep, April's dad, mom, and older brother would take turns touching me." When my mom switched to a different babysitter, the babysitter's sons would fondle her. Later, the babysitter's boyfriend joined in.

When my mom was in her early teens, my grandmother married a horrible man, who maliciously beat and raped my mom repeatedly. My mom spoke up and told her mother. Grandma said, "Quit making things up for attention." My mom ran away from home at thirteen years old. She tried to finish high school while working a full time job, but eventually dropped out of school so she could afford to live.

Before dropping out, my mom and dad met. In 1981, Mom gave birth to my sister, Jennifer who only lived a few hours. She had hydrocephalus. After they lost my sister, my mom finally agreed to marry my dad. In 1983, she gave birth to me. Shortly after returning home from the hospital, she locked herself in the bathroom with me for hours for fear that someone would hurt me. She later told me, "Everything I went through, I tried to protect you from." Growing up, I was concerned for her emotions and constantly tried to *mother* my mother. If she was upset, I would try to be a good girl and not cause too much trouble. She had trauma far beyond my understanding, but despite all of her suffering, she was a good mom who did everything she could for her family.

Dad spent most of his time working at the local mill or as a bartender before joining the military. Once he had a family to support, he worked tirelessly to take care of us. Unfortunately, my dad wasn't around much growing up. In the military, he worked sometimes sixteen hour days plus weekends. He was a very driven man who did what it took to allow his family to have a great life.

My parents knew that Josh and I were getting into trouble, but thought we were being "normal teenagers." My mom and dad were focused on work and didn't see a lot of what we were doing. Both my brother and I began to spiral. Before we completely crumbled, my dad received orders to move again. This time we went back to Idaho.

Life was different when we moved back. My friends had changed and I had changed. Honolulu, Hawaii was a large city and Post Falls, Idaho was a small town. I didn't resemble my old friends any longer. In school, girls would say, "The city girl thinks she's too good for us now." This of course wasn't true. I made a few friends, but if they weren't in school, I ate lunch in the library to avoid sitting by myself. I didn't want to seem like a "loner," or hear the rude comments of the girls in school.

Moving back to Idaho was awful. I began to look for ways to handle my emotions without confronting them. I did more drugs and went to more parties. The friends I did make didn't attend my school. There were a handful of people I could count on and one of them was the boy I had a crush on at the skating rink, Steve.

I could still depend on Steve. We started spending a lot of time together and became inseparable. I was sixteen years old when Steve and I started dating. I would rush home after school, then drive over to his house so he and I could cuddle while watching a movie. His mother would always interrupt, "Go home, Michelle, it's midnight!"

After dating for a short time, we wanted to become more intimate with each other. We were at a party one night where things got a little hot and heavy. We ended up having sex for the first time in the bathroom. Not a special location, but it was special enough to me. We weren't perfect, but he was mine and I was his. We both agreed, "We are going to spend the rest of our lives together."

In February 2001, my mom developed Acute Respiratory Distress Syndrome (ARDS). I took her to the hospital where she was immediately admitted. She went into a coma where she had her first stroke. She stayed in the medical center for two months. During that time, my dad had a hard time handling all of their personal affairs. I remember sitting at the living room table with him with bills spread from corner to corner. I put my big girl pants on and tried to help as much as I could.

My mother eventually recovered and in the summer of 2002, Steve and I moved in with each other. I was only eighteen years old. I forged Steve's signature on the lease agreement because Steve wasn't sure he wanted to move in yet. We talked about the possibility of getting married and having children later on in life, so I thought moving in together was a good idea.

Our house was "the party house." Every night we had people over drinking and playing video games. I remember waking up at 2 a.m., walking into our living room, with people sitting around the TV drinking beer and playing *Halo* on the Xbox. This was a big problem for me.

I was in my first year of college and these late night parties started a number of fights between Steve and me. I never finished school and when I was twenty we moved to Los Angeles so I could take a stab at an acting career. L.A. was a large, glamorous, exciting city that was both alluring and enticing. As soon as we got settled, we found jobs; me as a waitress and Steve in phone sales. The problem with Los Angeles is that it is easy to fall prey to the party life.

Steve and I went to clubs, drank alcohol, smoked weed, and did cocaine. Most nights, we came home from work, watched Jay Leno and smoked a joint with friends. This cycle was repetitive for almost three years. Needless to say, I wasn't moving forward with my acting career.

One night my dad called me and said, "Your mom is dying, you need to come home, Michelle." He encouraged me to move to Portland where they were stationed. She was having Transient Ischemic Attacks (TIA) that would debilitate her for days. After the attacks, she had immobilizing migraines and would have to stay in her room until they passed.

Transient ischemic attacks are often labeled "mini-strokes," though they are more accurately characterized as "warning strokes." The only difference between a stroke and TIA is that with a TIA the blockage is temporary, not permanent. It was suggested by my mom's physician that she needed to take better care of herself and limit stress. My dad and I agreed I needed to come home to help.

My mom started to improve after Steve and I relocated to Portland. Unfortunately, my relationship with Steve ended shortly after the move. He and I were growing in two different directions and we weren't compatible any longer. I was approximately twenty-four years old when we broke up. Steve and I are still friends to this day.

Shortly after the break up, I started dating a very attractive man named Richie who worked at the same restaurant I did. He had dark hair, big brown eyes, and beautiful tan skin. He was a school teacher during the day and a bartender at night. He enjoyed living life to the fullest and I was attracted to his carefree nature. We worked all day and partied all night.

I frequently went with the flow, even if they were idiotic. I remember being on vacation with Richie in Cancun, walking through the stores trying to buy drugs. Not a very smart thing to do in a foreign country with the cartel around. Richie and I had our fair share of experiences with illegal drugs. My addiction to cocaine began as an innocent habit that quickly grew into an every other day obsession. I was spiraling downhill quickly.

I remember lying in bed after a long night of doing cocaine. My heart was pounding out of my chest and my mind racing. My body couldn't relax, and I sure as hell couldn't sleep. This was like any other night for me and Richie; we would get out of work and invite our friends over to play poker or shoot darts. I had a Lazy Susan in the middle of our kitchen table where we would put a plate, a hundred dollar bill, a card and a few grams of cocaine. The nights were long, entertaining, and sleepless. I didn't think I was doing anything wrong because I had a good paying job, a boyfriend, a small business, and I was looking into buying a home.

But I was screaming inside. That night, while tossing and turning in bed, I spoke to the ceiling fan. "I need help and if anyone is out there I promise I'll stop, just help me." I begged the invisible ears and eyes surrounding me for forgiveness. I heard a response I wasn't expecting.

I heard God's unfamiliar voice tell me that it was alright, that I was loved and that He would take care of me. I began questioning who God was after this experience. My faith in Christ began at the start of 2010. At first I was extremely skeptical, like a person sitting in a large conference room hearing a time share presentation by two overly pretentious, smiling people. I would listen to the sermons, but I didn't jump in with two feet. I was reluctant to give up my lifestyle and change. I thought that I needed to be perfect, but I learned that wasn't true and Jesus loved sinners. I was still partying, but the pace was slowing. I joined a woman's study group where I came in hungover, with the smell of whiskey still on my breath, but the ladies accepted me, loved me, and always greeted me with a smile. Angie said, "I'm glad you joined us, Michelle. Where would you like to serve today?"

Slowly but surely, I started going to church regularly. I felt welcomed, acknowledged, and loved. I began volunteering with the babies every Sunday morning, still occasionally smelling like the night before. Life was starting to look more like a beautiful journey rather than a bent corkscrew. I was baptized on Easter

Sunday in 2010. God became a large part of my life and I began limiting my involvement with people who could gain access to drugs, including Richie. With God's help, I ultimately beat my addiction.

Although I am far from perfect, I try to do what is right. There have been slip ups here and there, but I always come crawling out of the holes I dig for myself. Drug addiction is a difficult habit to kick. Typically, people need rehabilitation programs and/or frequent meetings to help them get over their constant urges. My brother, for example, served a five-year sentence in a state penitentiary because of a methamphetamine addiction. Josh is struggling with meth to this day and I support him and love him the best I know how. I adore my brother and I know one day he will conquer his addiction.

Isaiah 6:9 states *"...You will hear my words, but you will not understand. You will see what I do, but you will not perceive its meaning."* I thought that because I found Christ, I would have no worry, fear, doubt, or hardships. That ideology is incorrect. Adversity, calamity, grief and suffering are all part of life. God continues to love me even through my sin. He understands the power of the flesh. He speaks to me, but sometimes I choose not to listen. Sometimes I block Him out when I need Him the most.

Chapter Two: Falling In Love

December 2011

I lived in the suburbs of Portland until August of 2011. I loved Portland, even though it rained every day. I loved going outdoors and hiking, feeling the warm rain on my face and the heat of the sun penetrating my skin. The smell of bell-shaped Oregon plum flowers, magnolias, dogwood, and cherry blossoms were always in the air. The city was cool and hip, full of unique individuals with buoyant personalities. Portland is known for great food and exceptional happy hours.

In the spring of 2009, while I was dating Richie, I worked for a national restaurant chain in Vancouver, Washington. An employee at the restaurant named Jonathan was involved in a business venture and approached me about a multi-level marketing company. Jonathan convinced me that my life could be much better than that of a waitress. He was tall, smart, and charming. I trusted Jonathan and decided to attend a leadership conference. "I promise your life will change, Michelle. You've got so much potential," he said. I listened to the visions of the leaders, and immediately bought into the dream of becoming something more. I had one-on-one coffee dates with friends and family to promote my new business endeavor. I bought all the necessary products and followed all the steps. I eventually learned this entrepreneurial business was a lot more difficult than the "successful" people led on.

In July 2009, I was introduced to a handsome young man at one of the large functions by a mentor of mine. I don't want to use his real name, so I'll call him Paul. When I first met Paul, I thought he was a bit arrogant, egotistical, and conceited, but very good looking. He was tall, had beautiful blue eyes, light brown hair, and a really nice ass. He was only twenty-three years old, but had a success story of his own.

Paul grew up in a small town in California with two siblings. His household was a typical middle class family unit; his mother and father both worked to pay the bills, and the kids helped out when they weren't in school. Paul knew he wanted something more, something better for his future family. He thought of how he could make a ton of money, travel the world, and live a lifestyle most people could only dream of. His dream led him to network marketing.

We sat next to each other in the convention center during the leadership conference. There were probably five thousand people in the room, but the only person I could hear talking was Paul. "So did I tell you how much money this thing is making me? I'm gonna be able to buy a yacht in the next few years and travel the world," he said. Paul spoke about all his accomplishments. He talked about the trips he was taking, the money he was making, and what he anticipated his future to look like. He was charming and funny, but very enamored with himself. We lived in two entirely different parts of the country; he in California and me in Oregon. I was not anticipating anything more than a casual friendship, especially because I was still involved with Richie.

We became acquaintances and saw each other when we made appearances at the same functions. He was entertaining. "Hey Michelle, you look great in those suspender dress slacks," he would say. I would laugh and reply with some smart-ass remark like, "I've got a boyfriend Paul, shut up!" I smiled and tried to ignore him. On occasion, we would go to Denny's together with a large group and listen to the leaders in the organization teach.

A short time after our introduction I quit the business. I quit because I couldn't seem to figure out how to make money. Every time I sat down with a new male prospect and invited him to a meeting, he assumed I wanted to date him. He went to a meeting or two with me, then completely bailed. "Oh, uhh, I thought you were interested in going out…I don't want to do this business thing with you unless we're dating" they'd say. "I have no interest in a romantic relationship with you because I already have a boyfriend," I'd reply. I stayed in the business for nearly two years before I quit. My communication with Paul dwindled and we lost contact with each other.

The summer of 2011, I decided to move back to Los Angeles. I was sober and single at this point. Richie and I had gone our separate ways and I was trying to figure out what I wanted to do with my life. My father retired from the military which left me with a few choices. I could move with my parents to Idaho, stay where I was in Oregon, or move back to Los Angeles. I was ready for a change and decided to try my cards at acting yet again. This was the second attempt at moving to Southern California to pursue a career in the entertainment industry.

I spoke with my boss at the restaurant I was working at and he told me he would give me a recommendation. "Of course I'll write something up for you; you've been a great employee," he said. Everyone thought it was a good idea for me to move back to Los Angeles. A few of my friends said, "We know you are gonna make it. You need to go." I even talked to my pastor and he suggested a new church to attend close to the San Fernando Valley. I loaded my car, sold most of my possessions, and drove down the coast to sunny Southern California.

I met a wonderful, charming, intelligent, silver-haired man named Dean through a mutual friend. He owned a home in the San Fernando Valley and allowed me to rent a room in his beautiful three-bedroom house. Dean's mother and father passed away shortly before my arrival, so Dean was delighted to have me move in. I was very lucky because finding a decent place to live that didn't cost an arm and a leg was unheard of in L.A. I started attending the church my old pastor recommended, found a job, and began the pursuit of my acting career. I very quickly got involved in classes, theatre, independent films, and I produced and starred in a play of my own. I thought I was on my way to becoming a viable, working actor and making my dreams come true.

I auditioned for a short film at the New York Film Academy in late 2011. I felt I aced the audition and wanted to find a way to get in contact with the director to thank her for the opportunity to star in her film. Although I wasn't cast, I decided to track her down and joined a social media website to look her up. Once I joined, the site obtained access to my personal information, email addresses, and various accounts. It sent messages to all of my contacts through email inviting them to join the website. Soon after, I received a reply from an old friend.

"Michelle, it has been sooo long, how are you..."

It was Paul from the multi-level marketing company I was involved in three years prior! The very handsome, narcissistic, pompous man wanted to resurrect our friendship.

"I am doing well. I moved to L.A. a month ago to go after my acting career. It is going great. I found an awesome church too. How are you? How is the biz?"

His reply was somewhat of a shock to me.

"I left the business because of some unfortunate circumstances that happened with my mentors."

He told me that he had other businesses that were doing well, which sparked my interest. He also said…

"Your profile picture is beautiful, are you single?"

I replied that yes, I was. I wanted to find out what Paul was doing with his life since our multi-level marketing days. I found out he was in real estate, was newly single, and was just as optimistic about his future as he had been three years earlier.

"I'm living in L.A. just trying to survive as a struggling actress and I have no desire to get into a relationship."

Paul had different intentions. We started talking and exchanging messages and he seduced me with romantic words of affirmation like, "You are absolutely amazing, Michelle, you inspire me." He'd tell me what an incredible actress I was, although he had never seen me perform. He looked me up online and commented on my photographs. "You are one of the most beautiful women I have ever seen." He kept imploring the idea of a relationship with me although I had extreme hesitation. We stayed in contact via social media, text, and phone until I agreed to meet him face to face. I guess his romanticisms paid off.

He didn't live far from Los Angeles and came down often for business meetings. On September 26, 2011, he was passing through the city and wanted to take me to lunch. I agreed and met him for sushi in West Hollywood. I was pleasantly surprised at how he had matured; Paul was aging well. He was stylish, suave, and well-dressed, with some added qualities including better conversational speaking and listening skills. He was 6'2" with bright blue eyes, a gorgeous, toned body, and he smelled like the perfect amount of sweat and Old Spice deodorant. I don't know why I didn't take notice of his very sexy physique three years earlier, but nonetheless, I noticed it now. He had great skin and straight white teeth. He was charming, captivating, and oh so alluring. I was physically and intellectually attracted to him.

I was in awe when I found out how successful he was. He started a business in 2010 that was booming. He said, "I started small in the world of real estate, then turned my company into a sizable threat to competitors." He was well on his way to making all of his dreams come true and his passion was infectious. I became enchanted by his desires and wanted to learn more about him.

Paul said he grew up in a home with challenges similar to many American families. From my understanding, his stepfather was emotionally abusive to him and his two younger siblings, and physically abusive to his mother. Although Paul never admitted to seeing his stepfather physically assault his mother, I learned violence occurred in the home on many occasions. His mother and stepfather separated when Paul was thirteen years old. Paul believed up until that point that his stepfather was his biological father. The shock of discovering the truth behind this lie sent Paul into a frenzy. Paul subconsciously blamed his mother for not telling him the truth for years. He used women as sex objects throughout middle and high school and never quite respected or appreciated the opposite sex. Paul self-medicated his anger with work and alcohol, leaving his condition to fester and build. He said, "I'm over all of that now, life must go on." I believed him.

Paul was a very persuasive man. He argued and manipulated for a living. He was able to make deals happen that most men could only dream of having the balls to achieve. I was very astonished and caught off guard by him. He pursued me with intensity. The attention he gave me was extremely flattering and gratifying. Paul asked me, "Where did you grow up? Are you close with your family and do you want a family of your own someday?" He really seemed to care about my desires. He sent me texts, was eager to please, and made me feel as if my existence as a human being was important to him. I woke up to flowers at the front door on many occasions with cards praising me on my excellence. Before going to bed each night, I would receive a message that said *"Goodnight, beautiful"* or *"Sweet dreams, sexy."* Every morning I awoke to another version of the evening text message. He was very sweet and I relished in the admiration I was receiving from him.

Paul wanted to take me out on an "official" date. He said, "I want to give you a night worth remembering, Michelle, please think about it." I didn't think I had the time for a full-fledged relationship because I was focused on starting my acting career, but Paul was compelling. He continued his praise and adoration of me. He advanced in his pursuit of me through flattery and gifts. I was starting to sway.

I flew to Idaho for Christmas 2011 to spend the holiday with my family. Paul and I were talking on a regular basis by this point and I considered him a good friend. My mom began asking me questions about my love life, as mothers do, and I told her about Paul. I said, "There's this guy that lives a few hours from me who sends me texts and we talk a lot." I told her that he wanted to pursue more than friendship with me but I didn't know if I wanted to since the reason I moved to L.A. was for the entertainment industry, not to find a man.

My mom interrogated me about my feelings. "What are your long term goals and why don't you want to try a relationship with Paul?" It was simple to her; there was a sophisticated, intelligent man seeking to have a romantic relationship with her daughter. "Why won't you jump in with two feet?" she asked. My mom wanted to see a picture of Paul, thinking perhaps it had something to do with his appearance. I asked Paul to send me a photo so I could show my mom what he looked like. Paul sent me a picture of him flexing in the reflection of a mirror in his bedroom. She looked at the photo, laughed, and said, "You should totally give him a chance, Michelle."

Paul and I had our first official date January 19, 2012.

Paul drove down to L.A and picked me up in his tan F250 truck around 3 p.m. As soon as he arrived, I was greeted with a kiss and a great big hug. I insisted on playing a game of Twenty Questions with him so I could learn even more about him. I asked, "What exactly do you do, I don't get it? How did you become so successful so young without the help of your family?" I asked about his mother and brothers, where he grew up, and specific details about what he wanted with his future. I said, "I want kids, do you?" I asked about the places he wanted to travel, and the qualities of the person whom he wanted to share his life with. Paul answered all my questions satisfactory. He eventually said, "Are you done yet, Michelle?" I smiled and stopped the game. He was smart and I found that trait extremely attractive.

I wasn't allowed to have guests over where I lived, so we drove to a hotel on the sunset strip in Hollywood where he had reserved two rooms. I told him, "I don't want to share a room with you." I insisted that if we had to share a room, I wanted separate beds. When we arrived at the hotel, the valet took his truck and the concierge asked if he could help us with our luggage.

We walked into a glamorous, bright, large one bedroom suite. This was my first time in a fancy hotel and I was excited. When I walked into Paul's hotel room, I was elated like a little girl. I scavenged the room, picked up all the novelties, and explored the itsy bitsy Grey Goose bottles kept in the mini bar. It was fun smelling all the lavender infused soaps and lotions. I was from a middle class family in a rural town. We never stayed at fancy hotels or took elaborate vacations. My parents, especially my dad, didn't understand why someone would pay anyone to park your car or carry your bags. My first experience in such a fascinating hotel was stimulating and exhilarating. It had only one problem; there was only one king-sized bed!

I told Paul, "I'm uncomfortable having only one bed." He said, "Don't worry about it, I'll fix it." He called down to the front desk to see if another room was available. We looked at a two-bedroom suite, but the price tag was $1,100 per night. I told Paul, "That's ridiculous, we'll see how the night goes and I can either get a cab or crash on the sofa instead." I thought it was foolish for him to spend so much money for one night in a hotel. We went back to our original room with one bed.

Paul decided we should go to a spa and get facials and massages before going to dinner. He took me to a place on Rodeo Drive in Beverly Hills. "This place is nuts," I said. It was fancy and super expensive! I thought aloud, "I'd never be able to afford this place." Paul heard me mutter and just laughed. I received a deep-tissue massage, had an exfoliating facial, and had my nails painted bright pink. I was being spoiled and it seemed as if he was enjoying pampering me. After the spa, we went to our hotel room to get ready for dinner.

He gave me privacy in the bathroom while I took a long, hot shower, lathering up my body and hair with lavender-infused soap and shampoo. I put on my cocktail dress, did my makeup, and walked out to the sitting area where Paul was waiting for me.

"You look stunning, Michelle," he said as he took me by the hand, and led me out the door.

We went to a five-star sushi restaurant across the street. Paul ordered us amazing food, saying to the server, "Bring us the Kobe Pepper, Yaki Niku and miso soup. Oh, and don't forget our drinks." For desert, we ate mango mochi and I had a chocolate martini. We walked across the street, back to the hotel, and spent the rest of the night laughing together at the bar in the downstairs lobby. I had a blast! Paul was charming and bewitching. I gave in to his seduction and stayed over at the hotel, not on the couch, but in the bed with him. I am not one to sleep with a man on the first date, but it happened.

From that point on, we were inseparable. I felt ecstatic to be in a relationship with such a caring, career-focused, attractive man. Paul drove to L.A. often during the first few months of our relationship. "Do you like the Dodgers and Lakers?" he asked. "I've never been to a professional baseball or basketball game," I answered. When he took me, I fell in love with the excitement in the stadiums. He was a huge sports fan, so we went to a number of basketball and baseball games in Los Angeles, San Diego, and San Francisco. He continued courting me with flowers, dinners and professional sporting events.

I started to fall in love with him and wanted to spend all my free time in his arms. I started day dreaming about marrying Paul and what our lives could look like together. One of my dreams was to aid developing nations and I dreamt Paul and I traveled the world together, helping children in third world countries. I imagined him proposing to me at a baseball game, or taking a plane to Italy on vacation to eat and drink wine. I was falling for him and falling hard.

One night, we were at a bar on the Sunset Strip in Hollywood and ran into a very powerful entrepreneur from New York City. Paul and this man started talking business and I was enamored with the sophistication and intelligence that Paul possessed. Paul said, "The housing market is gonna hit rock bottom and new-home construction will increase dramatically; we will make a ton of money." The conversation went on for hours and I learned a great deal about Paul and his business ventures. The two men talked about stocks, the capital required to make specific deals happen, and the real estate market. I remember being awed by him and inspired by what he said. He spoke of my desires with the same fervor, making me feel like I could accomplish anything.

According to Leslie Morgan Steiner, a domestic violence survivor, an American author, blogger, and businesswoman, abusers start by idolizing their victims and making their victims believe that they are the dominant ones in the relationship. Abusers want to know about your dreams, aspirations, passions, hopes, and family. Using Mrs. Steiner's words, Paul was creating a "magical relationship of trust" between us. He would confess to me his inner most personal fears and failures and praise me on my perseverance in life. Paul was idolizing me. He spoke highly of everything I wanted to do with my life and boosted my self-esteem. He said, "You can accomplish anything you put your mind to, Michelle." In a relationship with a healthy individual, praise is natural and acceptable; in an unhealthy relationship, that praise is later used as a weapon to put down or subdue the victim. My lack of healthy boundaries eventually enabled Paul to succeed with lifting me up then tearing me down, but that wouldn't come until later.

Chapter Three: The First Fight

March 2012

I was involved with my church heavily when Paul and I started dating. I served with youth, attended service every Sunday, and went to weekly dinners with people from the congregation. When I spoke to my friend Angie during dinner one night, I remember getting feelings of insecurity and uneasiness regarding my new relationship with Paul. "It sounds like Paul is being a complete fake," she said. Angie told me that although Paul was praising me, it seemed like he was narcissistic because of how often he talked about himself. Angie was very spiritual. She was beautiful, with dark curly hair and big brown eyes. "No relationship is perfect and Paul seems like he is trying too hard to maintain the illusion of perfection," she said. I appreciated her concern and I began questioning his praise.

Sometime after speaking with Angie, I met my friend Katie for lunch. She was an intelligent dark-haired beauty. I told her, "I really feel like Paul is the one." Katie was skeptical, but said, "As long as you're happy."

Out of nowhere, I distinctly heard God say "NO!" I chose to ignore my instincts and completely disregarded God's word. I thought perhaps it was my insecurity telling me I was just scared of getting into a relationship. I followed my heart instead of listening to the loud voice in my head.

The first time I drove to see Paul, I met him at one of his construction sites. He was tearing down a home with demolition bits and chisels. I watched as Paul lifted heavy equipment and swung a large hammer at the living room wall. He was drenched with sweat and had a boyish grin on his face while listening to his iPod. I wondered what song was playing and if I should sneak up on him.

Before I could make my move, he saw me and stopped what he was doing. He ran to me and said, "I don't always help my crew, but I wanted to show you what it takes to make money." He walked me through the rubble and talked about where new walls were going to be built and what he wanted the backyard to look like. I watched Paul with amazement. I respected his work ethic and admired his determination. I thought, "How could I question Paul, he seems like the perfect man for me." After he finished work for the day, he took me to a sushi restaurant in town.

We went back to his place after desert. Paul took me to his bedroom and began passionately kissing me. During sex that night, he stopped and said, "You know how much I love you?" He held me and caressed my skin. "I want to spend the rest of my life with you, Michelle."

I was so happy. I replied, "I'd do anything for you, Paul."

Afterward, we watched his favorite movie, *Top Gun*. "You look like Kelly McGillis. You're like my own private instructor," he said, teasing, which made me laugh.

I'm a hopeless romantic and Paul's words made me believe he was my Prince Charming. I thought he was the ideal man that I prayed for all my life. Up until this point, everything about our relationship felt like a fairy tale. I fell in love with him and didn't want to let him go.

March 2012 marked approximately two months since Paul and I started dating. I produced a play called *Proof* about a young woman who was gifted in mathematics and afraid she was going clinically insane. I was also the lead. March 15th was the last scheduled performance of the play and I invited Paul to come watch. It was a very dramatic role and one of the best, most rewarding performances of my career. I was enthusiastic that the play would open doors for other opportunities in the entertainment world.

When Paul arrived at the theater he seemed like he was off in some distant land. Paul spent the majority of his time on his phone while the crew set up the stage and the cast prepared for curtain call. "Perhaps it's an important work call," I told one of the cast members. Once the play began, Paul hung up the phone but continued to have a look of disappointment and boredom on his face. I did my very best and tried to show Paul how gifted I was. He didn't offer congratulations or a "good job" after we wrapped.

When the cast and crew finished tearing down the set Paul said, "Let's invite everyone back to my hotel for drinks." I agreed and gave directions to the hotel for anyone who wanted to go. Paul offered to drive a few people, but everyone wanted to take their own cars. I got in his black BMW 6 Series and on our way to the hotel I asked him, "Well, what did you think?" He told me that producing the play was a waste of my time. "There were only five people in the audience and your talent was wasted on an unsuccessful run of a play that no one will ever see," he said. I remember feeling sad, upset, and inadequate compared to Paul and his grandiose accomplishments.

At the hotel bar, he bought the entire team drinks and invited everyone up to his room to continue the party from his mini bar. The team had a great time. We were laughing and getting pretty intoxicated. Other patrons of the hotel called the front desk to complain about the noise. When hotel staff called the room Paul said, "I pay good money to stay at your hotel.The party will be over soon." I don't think they liked his comment very much, but allowed the party to continue for another hour.

All was going smoothly until the photographer for the play took me into the restroom to share her opinion of Paul. Stephanie was a good friend of mine. She was tall with brunette hair and a contagious smile. She and I starred in a movement play together six months prior to my rendition of *Proof.* Stephanie was an atheist and I enjoyed having conversations with her and her husband of nine years about their disbelief in God. Although I consider myself a Christian, I like to hear other people's opinions.

Stephanie confessed to me that Paul gave her the "heebie jeebies." She said, "Paul is not a good man and you should end the relationship now while you still can." I was stunned. She encouraged me to get out immediately. "He is manipulative, possessive, and self-centered. I know his type and Paul is dangerous," she said. She saw red flags such as controlling, money obsessed and self-absorbed. I said, "Paul is a wonderful man who loves me and appreciates me." I listened to her rebuttal, but couldn't believe what she was saying. I argued with her that Paul was everything I had ever wanted and she was wrong. She just shook her head and said, "Let's go back to the party."

When the cast and crew left for the evening, Paul grew very distant from me. I asked him, "What's wrong with you?"

"I heard everything that Stephanie told you, Michelle!" he replied. He was very upset. I cried and told him that I disagreed with her opinion. I fiercely tried to convince him that I didn't believe what she said. "I've never felt more disrespected by a woman in my life! I don't know if I want to be with you because you didn't stand up for me," Paul said. I told Paul he was a great man and Stephanie didn't know what she was talking about. Paul then had the audacity to say, "Well, Stephanie is easy and if I wasn't faithful to you, I could have had sex with her right here in this hotel room." He said Stephanie was saying seductive, intimate things to him and was trying to have an affair with him. Paul twisted the conversation so much that I questioned her intentions and integrity. Paul led me to believe that Stephanie was telling me to end it with him so she could have him. He gave me an ultimatum...him or her.

The next day I contacted Stephanie to talk about what happened that night. She emphatically told me, "Paul is lying. He is a two-faced, condescending ass, and I don't want to be around him, let alone sleep with him!" Stephanie asked me why I would ever think she would want to cheat on her husband of nine years. I wanted to believe her because she was my friend, but I also wanted to save my relationship with Paul. Paul insisted that if I chose him, I needed to end my friendship with Stephanie. I felt as if I were in the middle of a rock and a hard place. I didn't want to lose either of them, but knew I had no choice if I wanted to stay with Paul. I chose…and I still miss Stephanie to this day. She was a really fun, adventurous girl. She and I shared many memories together. I miss her easy going attitude and her constant encouragement. Stephanie didn't take the separation well. She was hurt, mortified, and dumbfounded. I felt terribly sorry.

This form of manipulation was the beginning of Paul's control over my friends. He continually voiced his opinion of the people I surrounded myself with, usually with criticism or disdain. He persuaded me to end specific relationships that he thought were unproductive. Paul insisted that his reasoning was right and I needed to listen to him and make appropriate changes. I allowed myself to distance from people I cared deeply about. I found myself questioning every relationship I had in my life and lost a lot of friends in the process.

A few weeks later, Paul asked me to come visit. I drove up anticipating spending a couple of romantic days together. When I arrived, he was still working and I ended up going to a coffee shop by myself in an unfamiliar town. I remember feeling frustrated and confused. He had me arrive at a specific time, but he was too busy to hang out with me. At the coffee shop, I had time to think. I wrote my first pros and cons list to help me gather my thoughts:

Pros	*Cons*
HOT!	*Swears a lot*
Will accentuate the red carpet well	*Too busy and does not have time for me*
We are a lot alike	*Sometimes disrespectful*

Advises me in business and finances	*Thinks what he does is more important than what I am doing*
Successful	
Won't cheat	*Tells me I have "rules"/ tells me what to do and how to do it*
Opens doors	*He lives too far away and won't move*
Says good things to me	*He will take time away from my career*
He loves me	*Not ready to marry*
Wants kids	*Makes me feel angry*
Great eyes, ears, face	*Never will be around*
Supportive of my dreams	*Wants me to do something besides acting*
Christian	*Doesn't attend church often if at all*
A dreamer	*People often tell me "Don't fuck with Paul."*
Smart	*Different lifestyles*
I am financially taken care of	*Different goals*
Loving when not overly stressed	*Incapable of time-management*
Young	*Young*

At the bottom of my list I wrote the following:

"What would another man be like?"

I began questioning everything in our relationship. I started to question Paul's ideas, opinions, and behaviors. Some of the warning signs that Stephanie told me to watch for were beginning to appear. Paul was starting to tell me to look at my life differently. He asked, "Why do you want to become an actress when it is so difficult to achieve that dream? It's a waste of your time." He suggested I think of something else to do with my life. He would praise me and put me down in one sentence.

"You are a very talented actress, but you will never be able to make it in the industry because there are too many women who look like you."

I was walking on egg shells to prevent any arguments. I thought I was putting everything I had into our relationship and I wasn't getting what I deserved emotionally. Although he spoiled me with lavish gifts, the praise and adoration were beginning to decline. I thought it was something I was doing wrong. I started blaming myself for his lack of sensitivity. I said aloud, "Maybe it's me?" I was troubled, anxious, tense, edgy and worried.

I don't know exactly why I didn't listen to the inner voice in my head saying something was wrong. Perhaps I fell for the illusion that Paul would be able to make my life perfect. Or maybe I was a sucker for staying in a dysfunctional relationship because I wanted to feel loved.

The warning signs were right in front of my face. I even acknowledged that things didn't feel right, but I believed all Paul's glorification and worship of me, not understanding what he was doing— manipulating me, conforming me to his way of thinking and being. I began to believe that my insensitivity was real and that Paul was always right.

After Paul finished his work on that visit, he apologized for his absence. We spent the weekend going to dinner, movies, and driving around town. "I love you, Michelle," he said on our way to the Regal Movie Theater one night. He held my hand and kissed me. His gesture made me believe everything would be okay. I needed to stop overthinking, I thought.

I noticed how beautiful his hometown was. I met his siblings, his mother, and some of his business partners. His mom was loud and a little rough around the edges. Her name was Kathy. She had short, brown, curly hair and squinty blue eyes. She smoked cigarettes and seemed like a hot mess. She said, "I hope this one lasts," while talking to Paul in her kitchen. She then looked at me and winked. I didn't know what to think, but I was happy she hinted that she liked me.

That weekend, Paul and I talked about the possibility of me moving in with him in. I entertained the idea. However, I didn't want to move from L.A. because it would take me away from the entertainment industry. I told him, "I'll think about it."

I was in love with Paul and wanted more than anything for us to work out. Falling in love and being fearful are a lot alike. They both give you that anxious feeling of butterflies in your stomach, a sense of excitement, and a general unease physically and mentally. It is easy to confuse love with fear. I thought I was in love.

Looking back, I realized I was scared for reasons yet to be known.

Chapter Four: The Devil Within

April 2012

To show me how much he cared, Paul decided to pay off my debt. I was roughly ten thousand dollars in debt on credit cards and he wanted to take care of it. Paul said, "There are no strings attached, I just want to do this for you." I was overwhelmed, excited and gracious for his generosity. He then asked me, "Could you add me to all of your credit cards so that we can have joint accounts?" I should have seen the red flags loud and clear, but I didn't. "We can use your credit cards for all of our expenses and then I will pay them off each month." He mentioned that he would increase my credit score by running up balances on all the cards then making large payments periodically. Theoretically, that process works, if the credit cards get paid off each month. At that time my credit score was already 780, but Paul swore, "I can make your credit even more impressive by using this strategy." I believed him and did as he asked.

According to many experts, an abuser will wager an insidious campaign to convince a woman that she needs him. Controlling a woman's finances is just one of many tactics that abusers use. According to the National Network to End Domestic Violence, "Financial abuse is a common tactic used by abusers to gain power and control in a relationship. The forms of financial abuse may be subtle or overt but in in general, include tactics to limit the partner's access to assets or conceal information." I believed Paul was sincere in trying to help me with my credit score, I didn't realize it was another tactic to control me.

One afternoon, we got into an argument while driving on the 101 Freeway heading south from his office. He said, "Do you understand what I do? You have a lack of respect for all I do for you, Michelle!" He believed that I didn't appreciate him and I needed to give him more commendation for what he accomplished and how he supported me. He stated, "You are a spoiled brat and don't deserve what I do for you!"

I argued with him. "You're wrong, Paul. I totally respect you and all your hard work," I said. I told him that I would do more to show him my appreciation. I began to cater to his every need as my act of atonement.

He did a very good job at manipulating my thoughts by his words of affirmation and then tearing me apart with contradictory statements. "You are a smart woman, but your lack of respect isn't going to be tolerated," he said. I was being controlled by him, and didn't realize it. His words stung. I started to believe that I was acting like a spoiled brat and I was in the wrong. I thought Paul was right and I needed to change. I pretended to be happy all the time to make sure not to upset him. I coddled him when he was upset and changed my schedule every time he needed. I assumed responsibility for his emotional health.

On the day of that fight, I was scheduled to work a bartending shift in L.A. that evening. I was supposed to leave his area by 2 p.m. to make it to work by 6 p.m. Paul said, "If you leave, you might as well never come back." He also said, "If you decide to leave, you can't take your things from my house." If I drove back to Los Angeles, I would have to leave my belongings with him and our relationship would be over. He threatened me, yelled at me, and made sure I "agreed" with his point of view.

"Without me you wouldn't be able to afford anything! If it wasn't for me, you would be broke and desolate."

He then forced me to call my boss to quit my job. Paul said, "You don't need to work since I pay for everything we do anyway." He told me to use our credit cards for all my expenses. He promised he would pay them and I wouldn't have to worry about money. He said, "I'm not going to allow you to go back to work. You should think about what you want to do with your life besides bartending and acting." Bartending would get me nowhere and acting was a waste of time, in his opinion. Not long ago, he had praised me for my acting ability and dreams. I was stunned by his statements.

"In exchange for not working, you can work for me," he said. He told me that I was to drive him to meetings, accompany him to dinners, help him decide final design concepts for his businesses, and manage all his personal needs such as making appointments and handling the bills. He wanted me to work for him as a personal assistant in exchange for his financial support. "You can think about what you want to do with your life while you take care of us," Paul said.

I involuntarily agreed. I quit my job because I didn't want to lose him. I wanted to maintain the illusion of happily ever after. He threatened me, but he also painted a beautiful picture of life without having to rely on a regular nine-to-five job. He justified me not working in a way that I desired. Paul said, "I will take care of you forever," and I believed him. He told me my dreams weren't realistic. He began replacing my ambitions with his own, making me believe I wanted the same things as him.

After I accepted his ultimatum, he apologized to me for letting his temper get out of control. "It's not fair that I pushed you into quitting your job when you weren't ready," he said. Then he spoke of all the wonderful things we could do together because I didn't have a job to dictate my schedule any longer. He illustrated a fantasy life where working wasn't necessary. He said things like, "Now we can travel whenever we want and you can spend time hiking." After fully embracing his apology, I bought into his idea of being a stay-at-home girlfriend.

I spoke to my parents three to four days a week. I couldn't tell my parents what was going on. I definitely couldn't tell them that I was forced to quit my job, so I said, "Paul offered to support me while I work on my acting career." I lied. My mom questioned me, but I kept up the false pretenses. I thought I could handle Paul without telling anyone the truth.

I stayed nearly every night at his house after I quit my job. The end of April 2012, Paul said to me, "I want you in a better car; your car is a piece of shit." I didn't argue with him. I was driving a beat up 1994 Saturn and he proposed a new Lexus. He told me, "Either sell your car of I am going to run it over with a bulldozer at my construction site." He actually wanted to crush my car with a CAT, but I sold it for $400 to one of my friends in L.A. who desperately needed transpiration. On May 3, 2012, he co-signed a lease on a new Lexus. He said, "I want your name on it as well so you actually own it." It was a four-door, eight-cylinder, blue speed machine. I loved the car and was super grateful.

The day we picked up the car from the dealership, I was supposed to drive to L.A. to make an acting class by 7 p.m. I knew I had to leave directly from the car lot in Santa Barbara in order to make it on time. "I want to drive the car home before you go to L.A. tonight," Paul said. I argued with him saying, "Traffic is going to be horrible by the time we get back to your house and I won't make my acting class!" He didn't care. His brother came to the dealership with us and Paul told him, "Drive my truck home because I'm going to drive the Lexus." I couldn't talk him out of his decision. As soon as we arrived back to his house, I immediately left. Traffic was so bad, however, that I turned around and drove back. "He knew I would get caught in traffic and made me purposely miss my class," I said aloud while driving up the 101. I hid my frustration when I reached the house. I figured he had just leased me a new car and I didn't want to seem like I was being a brat.

When I walked in, Paul said, "Hey, sorry you missed your class, but since you don't have to go to L.A. anymore, we should go to dinner with Melissa and Jordan." I agreed and got ready. I drove us to the restaurant in my new car. Paul was on his phone finishing some work from earlier in the day when I pulled into a parking space. He looked up and asked, "Are you stupid or do you even care about the car I just fucking bought for you?" I parked the car in a very tight space, which triggered him and he started screaming at me for my incompetence. I was stunned. He then said, "You should have found a different fucking parking spot because the car is going to get scratched." He continued insulting me for my inability to process that information and implied I was ignorant and foolish. "You don't deserve a brand new vehicle if you are going to be so dumb to park it next to a beat up pickup truck!"

I said I was sorry and I didn't deserve to be screamed at because of such a small mistake. Paul's anger only intensified. He repeated his verbal attacks until I moved the car to another parking spot. He said, "I'm disappointed that I can't trust an almost 30-year-old woman with a fucking car. I should have left you in your damn Saturn!" I tried to reason with him and apologize for not thinking about the car being scratched. He didn't stop his verbal attack until I said, "It was totally my fault, won't happen again, I'm sorry."

The car represented his power over me in a number of ways. Later in our relationship, I wasn't allowed to drive the Lexus without his permission and only if he didn't need it. Paul's schedule was more important than anything else I had going on, in his opinion, so he always got first dibs. The car symbolized control in a deeper sense; he was beginning to regulate everything in my life.

I was a bit shaken when we walked into the restaurant to meet his friends. I got teary eyed and had to excuse myself from the table to calm myself down. I was humiliated and wounded by his tantrum. Melissa sensed something was wrong and came into the bathroom to make sure I was alright and to smooth out the situation. Through tears I said, "Paul had a stressful day at work and didn't mean to yell at me." I justified Paul's verbal attacks and said he unintentionally took his anxiety out on me. Once we got back to the table, Paul glared at me for making a scene. He ordered food and drinks for us and never mentioned me crying in the bathroom. He didn't acknowledge his handling of the situation or how it affected me.

Many people who experience abusive language as children tend to use it as grown-ups. Paul was used to being yelled at as a child, automatically assuming that was the proper way to handle confrontation as an adult. For punishment, Paul's stepfather used to make Paul kneel on grates and stay in a corner of a room for hours until he "learned his lesson." Paul made me feel worthless just as Paul's stepfather made him feel when he was young.

After dinner we went downtown to a local night club where the drinks began flowing. At the club, a guy asked me to dance and I accepted his invitation, primarily because I was hurt by Paul's previous remarks about my intelligence and I craved attention from someone who accepted me. Paul looked at me sadistically and said with mere disgust, "Quit acting like a slut."

My initial reaction was to slap Paul, and slap him hard. He disrespected me again and I didn't want to be demure and meek any longer. I felt as if Paul was taking my control away from me and I needed to assert myself, showing that I was not obedient and submissive to his every need. I slapped him because I thought it would get him to understand that I couldn't take the emotional abuse any longer.

I understand I was the first person in the relationship to lay a hand on my partner, the first one to become physically abusive, and I regret that. I know I could have handled the situation better, but in the midst of things, I let my temper get out of control. What Paul did in return was immensely more disturbing.

Paul thought it was the man who asked me to dance that slapped him. He started a fight with the guy and punched him in the nose, causing us to get thrown out of the nightclub.

Once outside, Paul grabbed me, pushed me, pulled my hair, and spit in my face. He said, "You should be left here without your purse or phone to think about what you just fucking did!" He expressed how I dishonored him and that our fight was all my fault. He said, "How dare you disrespect me in my hometown." That's when he kicked me while I was on the ground sobbing. He spat in my face at least three more times while in the parking lot, cursing and calling me a piece of shit and a whore. Paul was so angry that when he yelled at me the veins in his forehead bulged. I was scared of him, scared of what he might do, scared he would actually leave me there alone, and scared I was the one who provoked the monster within. He was successful in making me feel ashamed and foolish. Paul injured my dignity and self-respect. I began to think I deserved this unfair treatment, that I was the one to blame.

Melissa—who was this cute, petite blonde—stepped in front of Paul many times trying to protect me. She was only about five feet tall, but was quick-witted. She argued with him saying, "Stop this, you are being such an asshole!" She disagreed with Paul about leaving me without my purse and car in a town that was unfamiliar to me. She got spit on a few times when Paul was trying to strike me. This back and forth between the two of them went on for hours outside the nightclub. In the midst of their argument, Paul repeatedly yelled, spit, and grabbed me. Eventually, I said, "It's all my fault, I'm so sorry." I apologized for setting him off and triggering him. I apologized for everything, trying to calm him down.

I thought Paul was super stressed because of work which caused him to mitigate misery on me. I thought he couldn't control his outburst because of the strain from his job. I thought that if I accepted the blame, he would stop and we would move forward without having any more arguments. I felt ashamed for slapping him and started believing I was the culprit of this incident, that if it wasn't for my misconduct we wouldn't have argued and he wouldn't have gotten physically abusive with me. I didn't understand or comprehend that this was just the beginning and the abuse was going to get worse.

I felt I was a dreadful, appalling person who somehow deserved this treatment. Although Melissa was there trying to help me, I felt very alone and confused. All the nasty, detestable language Paul used hurt me to the core. Every time Paul spit on me, I felt like an abused dog in a puppy mill. And like that abused dog, I limped back to my owner.

I began to get lost in Paul's clutch. His grip on my mind grew stronger and stronger. I felt discombobulated and puzzled at what was happening. My thoughts weren't making sense to me. All logic was gone and I thought I could sooth Paul's hysteria by telling him what he wanted to hear, "It's not your fault, it's mine." By doing so, this caused him to feel that his actions were justifiable. That pulling my hair, pushing me to the ground, and spitting on me was legitimate retribution for slapping him. Towards the end of the assault, I started to believe that also.

We ended up staying at a nearby hotel in town instead of driving home. I stayed awake most of the night thinking about what happened, questioning if it was my fault. I told myself that Paul was extremely busy with his business and he had complications in his professional and personal life that made him snap. He had a rough childhood and I should have known better than to upset him, I thought. I made every excuse for his behavior. He never apologized for his actions because he believed I was the instigator of the fight. He only said he was sorry for spitting on me.

Paul and I met Melissa and Jordan for lunch the next day. In confidence, Melissa told me she didn't want anything to do with Paul any longer and didn't trust him. She asked me, "Can you tolerate this treatment for the rest of your life, Michelle?" I didn't know what to say. I took the blame for the fight, saying it wasn't his fault. Melissa said, "I think Paul needs intensive treatment because of the way he treated you, you know it's only going to get worse." I excused his actions and didn't believe Melissa.

I pushed away the people I knew could help me. I lied to my family and friends. I lied to myself. Paul was an emotional manipulator, he took no responsibility for himself or his behavior. It was about what everyone else did to him. Melissa stopped coming to the house and Jordan limited the time he spent with Paul after this incident.

One especially sinister form of control is called "gas lighting." John M. Gottman is a professor emeritus in psychology known for his work on marital stability and relationship analysis through scientific direct observations. In *The Domestic Violence Sourcebook*, he and his partner Dr. Neil Jacobson said the man convinces the woman "she is going insane by systematically denying her experience of reality and contradicting her experiences—especially of his abuse—until she begins to doubt her own sanity. This, they believe, may be the ultimate form of abuse—to gain control of the victims mind." Paul was beginning to become successful in this form of control. He was so intelligent and persuasive that I was beginning to give credence to his actions and words. I was questioning whether things happened the way I remembered or the way he explained them to me.

Paul had the audacity to command me to write a letter to him explaining why I got out of hand and to illustrate why he should stay with me. I felt a burning desire to tell him to go to hell, but I didn't. I gave him what he wanted. The letter I wrote consisted of loving words and sentiments, an explanation as to why I overacted, and projected future dreams of how our life could be together. I hand wrote thirteen pages and gave it to him.

He never read it.

<u>Chapter Five: Living With A Monster</u>

June 2012

Matthew 16:26 states, *"How do you benefit if you gain the whole world but lose your own soul in the process?"* I was losing myself. I lost my friends, my job, my congregation, my career and my freedom. My life was more about Paul than it was about me. I did everything based on his schedule, his wants and his desires.

At this point, we were not living together. I could have run away, I could have ended the relationship right there, but I didn't. I allowed him to treat me the way he did because I thought I could handle it and he would eventually change. I also thought I could help him. I believed he would realize his treatment of me was unfair and learn a better means of communication. I struggled with the possibility of leaving and began believing that the grass wasn't greener on the other side. So I stayed.

I learned later that changing him was unrealistic. Nobody was going to change simply because I wanted them to change. I loved Paul the best I knew how and hoped that would inspire him to change. Paul didn't think he was doing anything wrong so he didn't have the motivation to make a change. Andy Warhol said it best, "When people are ready to, they change. They never do it before then, and sometimes they die before they get around to it. You can't make them change if they don't want to, just like when they do want to, you can't stop them."

Shortly after the incident at the nightclub, Paul decided that I should move in with him. I wanted our relationship to work so I neglected my feelings. I questioned all the things I believed and wanted. I moved boundaries, adjusted my thinking, and countlessly corroborated his stories so they would become my own reality. He broke through my barriers and limitations. I thought he could give me everything I had always wanted; the love, the emotional commitment, and the lifestyle, even in the midst of our challenges.

He could be my fairy tale prince rescuing his princess from a wicked witch. Little did I know, Paul *was* the wicked witch.

Someone once said to me that life is not a fairy tale. If you lose a shoe at midnight, you're drunk, not a princess. I thought once we lived together he would change, that I could change him, a thought many people believe in romantic relationships. On May 26, 2012, I packed a U-Haul and drove north up the 101 Freeway to his hometown and my new home.

Paul already had a roommate when I moved in so he could offset his expenses and have help paying the mortgage. The night before I drove a completely packed moving truck to my new home, Paul blacked out due to severe intoxication. According to Paul and his friends, he broke almost all the furniture in his house, kicked in the door of his roommate's bedroom, and caused quite a ruckus. I had no idea this happened until I arrived at the house the next afternoon.

When I showed up, the inside of the home looked like a combat zone. There was broken glass on the Pergo hardwood flooring in the living room, dining area, and kitchen. Garbage bags were full of broken pieces of the kitchen table, coffee table, end tables, appliances and electronics. I asked about a piece of wood stuck in the ceiling above where the dining room table used to be located and Paul shrugged it off and said, "It's just another piece of the chair I broke." There were holes all over the drywall in the house. He had punched and kicked walls, doors and broke surfaces in the home. His tantrum finally ended once he started to sober up, many hours later.

He employed his friends to clean the house, pick up the broken furniture, and fix the door he kicked in. I remember sitting down on a broken chair in my new home looking around, watching the boys pick up rubble, thinking to myself, "What and who am I getting myself involved with?" I left my friends, my career, and my home to move in with the man of my dreams, or the person I thought was the man of my dreams. I had no friends, no family, and no community in my new city, only Paul. Because the boys were busy cleaning up Paul's mess, I unloaded the U-Haul by myself. I was able to unload almost everything, but the items I couldn't lift, Paul's brother helped me unload the next day.

Isolation is the next step in the cycle of domestic violence, according to Leslie Morgan Steiner. I was solely dependent on Paul. I asked his permission to buy plane tickets to see my family and asked his permission to befriend people, making sure they were acceptable in his eyes. I was constantly criticized for the amount of money I spent at the grocery store and told, "You can't buy this much crap!" Paul questioned me often, "What do you do all day?" And I heard regularly, "You are so fucking lazy." I was not only dependent on him as my only contact in a new town for social interactions, but financially as well. I had no job since he coerced me to quit my existing employment, and it was understood that I couldn't go back to work. Paul said, "I will supply you with whatever you need."

The one thing I needed was a reliable source of transportation. Paul would hardly let me drive my car, the one he had leased for me just a month earlier. He made me sell my reliable Saturn to upgrade to a new Lexus that I rarely was allowed to drive! He gave me one of his work trucks to drive around town when I needed to go anywhere. It was a 2008 Ford F250. If the truck would have been taken care of, it would've been fine. The truck, however, had no rear view mirror, no air conditioner, no radio, no backseat, and was completely gutted. The vehicle needed new tires and it often slipped when it rained. The tailgate was a rope, not an actual part of the truck, so if I went to the dump or did any shopping, I'd have to be very careful and drive slow so the items wouldn't fall out. Paul told me, "I don't think you deserve to drive your car since you don't appreciate what I do for you."

His roommate was a guy named Peter, who was an intolerant, mean, childish person. He was only about 5'4" with dark squinty eyes and black messy hair. I never saw him without a beer in his hand, wearing the same clothes as the night before. There were times Peter and Paul would sit and make fun of me while we watched a movie or I made dinner. Peter would tell Paul, "Michelle doesn't deserve you, you should go find another bitch." Peter told me many times, "Once Paul is finished with you, he's gonna get rid of you and find another chick to bang." Women were easily replaceable to him. I was pushed over the edge twice with his nasty remarks and poured my drink over his head. Paul laughed and thought it was amusing. Paul didn't do anything to help me, or to stop Peter's slander. He said, "You're a big girl, Michelle, you can handle it." Peter and I eventually figured out how to get along, but it took a while.

One Saturday afternoon before we left for brunch, Paul was on edge for no apparent reason; he was distant and uncommunicative. I had no idea what was wrong. Peter and I went with him to a seaside restaurant for food and drinks and I made a joke at the table to try and get his attention.

"You wanna know why Peter picks on me so much? Because he has secret feelings for me and is just waiting for you to leave the picture."

Paul didn't appreciate being the entertainment and said, "Why the fuck would you say something so stupid, Michelle?" He scolded me like a child. I was trying to loosen Paul up, but it didn't work.

The three of us walked to the bar on the other side of the restaurant after eating and had a few drinks. I think Paul had about five Vodka Red Bulls and began to show signs of intoxication. He was slurring and being obnoxiously loud. When we got back to the house, he and I started to argue. Paul said, "I felt so disrespected by your fucking comment at brunch, Michelle. Why the hell did you say that?" He called me a slew of inappropriate names. "You're a whore and a condescending bitch." He then pushed me so hard against the wall in our bedroom that my head went through the drywall. Actually, my head didn't go all the way through the wall, just bounced and made a significant dent. Paul said, "You deserve to be pushed around." His violence was somehow something I caused, he argued.

At this time in my life, I was confused and discouraged. I actually thought I was at fault for the constant slander and abuse. People have asked me, "Why didn't you leave then?" I answer as truthfully as I can. "I didn't think I could leave. I honestly thought things were going to get better if I stuck it out. I was waiting for him to realize what he was doing and fix his behavior."

I made excuses for his behavior and never brought up the physical violence from that Saturday afternoon. I asked Peter to help me patch the hole in the bedroom so people wouldn't ask questions if they came over. Peter asked me, "Why would you put up with this, Michelle?"

My response was, "But I love him. I know he'll change!"

Peter moved out a few weeks after this incident. He noticed how Paul's attitude and behavior were gradually getting worse. Peter wanted nothing to do with it. On Peter's way out the door, he looked at me and said, "Have fun with him." I thought Peter was an ass, so I took most of his comments with a grain of salt, but this one stuck. *What did he mean by this?* Peter found me on social media a few years later and we briefly spoke about my experience. He told me, "I was trying to warn you."

After Peter moved out, Paul said, "Now we can have our own space without Peter." He knew I was struggling so he added, "Things will get better now." I believed him, but Paul started to insult me more and more with each passing day. With his praise there was criticism. I was being brainwashed to believe I was stupid, lazy, incompetent, and helpless without him. He said, "You would be nothing if it wasn't for me." He'd come home from work and I'd walk on eggshells to try not to upset him in any way.

I've never been one to cook, but I made sure I had supper ready for him every day at 6 p.m. There were many times he wasn't satisfied with dinner and decided to order pizza or go out after I spent all afternoon prepping. He'd say, "I don't really feel like this tonight," and throw away the meal I cooked without any consideration of my time or energy. I taught myself new recipes so he'd enjoy dinner more and I became a pretty good cook. He rarely stopped working during our meals or acknowledge me for my hard work in the kitchen. He started to expect this every night and would get furious if the food was cold because he was late getting home.

During this juncture, I wrote in a diary I carried with me wherever I went. I needed an outlet for the emotional abuse I endured. One passage I wrote to Paul around June 1, 2012 read:

"Paul...

I don't know how much more I can show you that I love you. We both have said and done things to one another that have caused severe hurt and confusion. I've always been free-spirited and center of attention LOL which isn't always good. Before you and I started dating, in previous relationships I would dance with other people alot- I always had a "no touch" rule. I was defiant when I looked at you and told that guy yes for a dance. It's not that I don't love you, it's me somehow subconsciously avoiding pain.

Paul, you are handing me everything financially on a plate. It all is a bit overwhelming. I've told you in the past that if you didn't have all this $ and your big dream was to be a manager of Vons, I would still love you and want to be with you. You have so many things on your plate and an influx of complications and difficulties with people in business and your personal life. I don't know how you do it. I fell in love with Paul Wright. I want to help you with everything and I also want you. I want you the way you are, but you are disappointed in me and others in your life, and I don't know what to do about it. I want you to be happy Paul.

Honey, I don't know what else I can do to make you satisfied. I have changed my physical location, quit my job, taken a very large step back from acting, try to clean house (LOL), run you around, and am working on completely changing the way I think and live life. I'm learning to live your mindset and world. I know what you want to say... "I don't want you to change for me. I don't want you to give up anything for me"

Well, Paul the things that I am changing are good for me and good for you. These are changes that needed to be made years ago and you just have the balls to tell me about them. Also, you should feel loved, feel wanted, and feel needed (not $ but spiritually) that you have a woman who loves you so much that she wants to re-adjust her thinking for you. I've never in my live just "Let Go." I am slowly transitioning that way.

You are an amazing, brilliant person. You will go very far in life, I just hope and pray I will be with you. You will one day be a wonderful father and husband. You love deep and I think you have been wounded so bad that it's hard for you to completely trust and let someone in. I know God gave me you, now I'm trying to figure out how to keep you.

Baby, I love you with all my heart and soul. I'm sorry I'm having challenges, it reflects badly. I also need to learn to relax, I need to learn that I don't need approval in order to feel worthy. I am making changes, many of which are definitely necessary.

I want you Paul. I will love you forever. I also want you to be happy, so if I'm not making you happy I'll let you be.

Remember, I'll do anything for you Paul."

I was apologetic for everything. I really felt that the words Paul spoke to me were true to some extent. I thought if I changed who I was, I would make him happy. If I adapted to his lifestyle and way of thinking, everything would work out.

I wrote another "Cons" list on June 25, 2012. I didn't have anything else to add to a "Pros" list:

He is disrespectful
We fight about everything
Tells me that I am not productive
Asks me "what do you do all day?"
Makes me feel worthless
He talks down to me
Doesn't understand how difficult he is
Doesn't understand how difficult the move is
Language
His things are more important
I am not able to pursue my dream
We argue about money

Most of the items on my list continued and got worse. There was one time when Paul got so upset the housekeeper didn't clean the baseboards and freaked out. He said to me, "You can't even manage the cleaners correctly. What the hell do you do all day?" I had no idea why he was mad at me when it was the cleaner's responsibility to wash the baseboards. The psychological impact of his words were starting to weigh on me. That afternoon when he was at work, I scrubbed the baseboards in the house. It took me four hours to get them clean.

On June 26, I wrote him an email while he was at the office:

"Paul,

You and I have had many quarrels; many of which are very hurtful and disrespectful. Outside of the fights, you and I laugh, giggle, flirt, and act like high school kids. You are the most determined, strong, dedicated, loving man I have ever met. I adore your work ethic, your constant dedication to your future family, and your desire to give. I'm sorry for all the bad that I have done, i.e. talking to biz people, causing fights while intoxicated, and causing a discrepancy between you, Jordan, and Melissa. I can move on from the hurtful language, the constant busy-ness, and the physical. If "us" is what you want we can and will flourish. Relationships have ups and downs. We complement each other on levels that are extremely important: religion, kids, future lifestyle, determination, etc., let alone we have the same scary movie, love cheesecake, like movies, and we make love really well. :-). I just wanna let you know that I want to be with you, for all that we are and all that we will become. I love and respect you Paul. I cannot wait for our weekend away for just the two of us. I look forward to spending my life with you..."

Paul constantly told me how much he loved me. It was difficult for me to end our relationship when I heard him say, "You are the world to me." Although he emotionally and physically abused me, the heartfelt words kept me in the vicious cycle.

Paul insisted on falling asleep watching television. I am not a sound sleeper and was kept awake by the blaring sound of the TV throughout every night. I begged and pleaded with him to shut it off, but he wouldn't, even after falling asleep. If I shut it off and he woke up, he would turn it back on. He said, "You have nothing to do tomorrow; you can handle a little noise." I learned to use ear plugs and cover my face with blankets in order to get some shut eye. There was no negotiating with him.

I remember I went to Best Buy and bought him a pair of wireless headphones, so he could watch his TV and I could sleep. He laughed at the idea and told me to return them immediately. He said, "I won't sleep with these damn things on my head, I'll look like a buffoon." I don't know why he was concerned with how he looked while sleeping, but I returned them nevertheless.

In July, I found a church in town I liked and started attending regularly on Sundays. Going back to church made me feel whole again. It was such a big part of my life in L.A. and I was grateful to have a community again. Paul went with me once and never went back. He told me, "It's a waste of time for you to go to that church. The entire congregation are hypocrites!" He said they were going nowhere with their lives, but if I wanted to end up like the people in church, I could attend.

I signed up for a woman's Bible study group immediately. I was the youngest person by twenty years, but I didn't care. I felt that I finally found somewhere I could escape from my dilemma. I would go every week and began sharing bits of my story in confidence with some of the elderly women. I said, "I know a girl who is living with a man who is not so nice to her, what should she do? She isn't going to leave." They encouraged me without telling me I was wrong. Many of them said, "He won't change honey, maybe you should really urge your friend to get out." I didn't disclose crucial information that would have raised suspicion, but I knew a few women understood what was actually going on.

There were times in the mornings before Paul had to be at the office that he would start screaming at me for something inconsequential. He started blaming me for everything wrong in his life from his business to personal affairs. "You're the reason Ronald messed up the deal. I was up too late with you and missed the damn meeting," he said. Ronald was his primary business partner. He was twenty years older than Paul with grayish hair and a friendly smile. Paul said to me, "All you like to do is sleep in every fucking day and do nothing. This is all your fault!"

Paul thought I should be doing something else with my time. I didn't have to be up when he did at 7 a.m, so I slept in. He wouldn't let me get a job. After he finished emotionally and verbally abusing me, he would sometimes skip meetings and stay with me all day long, saying "I'm so sorry for yelling at you."

None of his business associates knew why he cancelled meetings. They brushed it off as his normal behavior. Paul was very good at keeping the abuse a secret. According to Jacobson and Gottman, at least 80 percent of abusers are non-violent outside the home. Paul was an upstanding citizen, helped kids, and went to leadership events. He coached people who were sometimes twice and three times his age. No one knew anything, not even Ronald.

A vast majority of batterers are only violent towards their female counterpart and often their children, rarely anyone else away from home. Dr. Lenore Walker suggests that many women who have lived through domestic violence, and professionals who study it, agree there is a sort of "Dr. Jekyll and Mr. Hyde" aspect to the man's personality. Abusers seem to have a split personality. Many are successful on the job, handsome, well-liked, charming and kind in public. Typically both sides are seen in the home but only the pleasant side is seen by the public. This fit Paul perfectly.

Chapter Six: The Ugly

August 2012

For my birthday, Paul wanted to spoil me. He told me, "You deserve a night in a hotel on the coast and a shopping spree, Michelle." I was anticipating a beautiful night at a super chic hotel after shopping at some of the boutique stores in town. I was excited and grateful as we drove to different shops purchasing clothes, shoes and accessories. I modeled an outfit for a rodeo he and I were planning to attend the next day. I twirled and said, "I look like a cowgirl now."

By the end of the afternoon, I think Paul spent around two thousand dollars. This was the first "shopping spree" he had taken me on and I learned very quickly he didn't like spending his money, even if it was his idea; he had a reluctance freely spending it. He told me, "I don't think people appreciate what I do for them." This included his friends, his siblings, his mother, and me. Paul immediately regretted going shopping and had buyer's remorse shortly after purchasing all my gifts. "We shouldn't have stopped at so many stores," he said. I responded, "We can return some of the things if you want." He shrugged it off.

After shopping, Paul drove us down the coast of California on our way to the hotel. It was an excruciating ninety-five degrees outside. The sun blazed over the ocean. The waves were a light turquoise with hints of crystal glimmer. I watched as the water crashed on the rocks of the bank. It was a breathtaking site. I said aloud, "What an amazing birthday."

Upon our arrival at the hotel, the valet parked our car and the concierge followed us to our room with our bags. We showered and dressed for dinner. Paul said, "I think we should take a cab since we both are going to be drinking." I agreed and called to the front desk to order us a cab. After we got dropped at the restaurant, our hostess led us to an outside table beside a gray cobblestone fireplace. It was a beautiful restaurant with marble countertops and an elegant ambiance.

Paul positioned himself across from me and proceeded to ignore me, looking on his phone at various social media websites for most of dinner. He was distant and unaffectionate and I had no idea why. I asked him, "What are you looking up?" He told me, "I've just got a few things to get done, Michelle." I assumed he was upset with me for some undeserving reason because of his lack of endearment. I made sure to be on my best behavior and not to cause a fuss.

After dinner, we went to a bar and met a few college-aged kids who were lively and entertaining. I *watched* the crowd dance––I was not allowed to dance after the nightclub incident where I slapped Paul. The music was a loud mixture of bass and screeching voices. I made a comment, "The cute girl in the tan suede boots makes me think of me when I was her age." She was drunk and dancing without a care in the world, very provocatively with little concern for anything. She was noticeably high on drugs and being very boisterous.

"I don't appreciate you mentioning what you used to be like when you were a drug addict!" Paul said. He dropped his glass in the middle of the dance floor and I watched it shatter into a thousand different pieces. He looked at me with fire in his eyes, grabbed my arm, and said, "We are leaving right now." I knew I was in trouble.

I had no idea why he was so angry with me. I was startled by his reaction. All I did was say someone reminded me of myself. It was an obvious comparison of who I used to be, of who I wasn't any longer. I felt I didn't deserve his attitude and aggression, especially on my birthday. Paul was being insensitive and careless.

He dragged me outside, gripping my arm with so much force I couldn't get away. He flagged down a cab and told me, "Get in." I didn't listen and tried to pull away from him. I squirmed and pleaded, "Paul, you're hurting me." I was unsuccessful; he held my arm tighter and pulled me into the cab with him. I was silent during the drive to the hotel and I was trying to figure out how to calm him down. I thought I triggered his appalling new mood. I caused his unrestrained anger somehow. I didn't fuss with him the entire drive thinking if I just listened and agreed with him, then he would stop, then we could go back to the club.

When we arrived back to the hotel, he started screaming at me because of my comment about the girl at the bar. He became so furious that he hurdled towards me in the bathroom, put his hands around my neck, and squeezed so hard I couldn't utter a single word. He pushed me up against the wall and started berating me.

"You disrespectful bitch, you don't deserve what I do for you!"

I couldn't breathe. I couldn't challenge him or articulate my point of view. Once he released my throat, I screamed as loud as I could. My vocal cords hurt, but I tried really hard to yell. I wanted someone to hear me. I was frightened that he would kill me. Paul stumbled towards me again, uneasy on his own feet because of all the alcohol he consumed, and said, "Shut the fuck up before someone hears you." He strangled me a few more times before a patron at the hotel heard my cries and called the police.

The cops showed up and banged on the front door. Paul looked at me before letting the officers in the room and said, "Don't say anything, Michelle, I don't want to send you to jail." He said I was at fault and if I said anything they were going to take me to jail, not him. The officers began interrogating both of us. They separated us, putting Paul outside and leaving me sitting on the bed. I had tears streaming down my face, my makeup was in disarray with black mascara and eye liner running down my cheeks. I was fearful if I told the police what happened, I would be taken to jail. I was sobbing hysterically

I could hear Paul trying to keep his temper at bay. He refused to say anything to the police. I was so scared and confused.

My throat hurt and my body hurt. I was heartbroken and discombobulated. I was scared that what Paul said about me going to jail was true. This delusion ran through my head while an officer kept asking me, "What happened?" I had never been in a situation like that before, and I had no idea how things worked when law enforcement got involved.

I eventually spoke through my hysteria. "He strangled me and I'm scared," I said. The officer wrote down my statement and took Paul to jail, not me. I'm surprised the officer was able to understand anything I said because I was so distraught. As soon as the patrol car drove away with Paul in the backseat, I crumbled to the floor. How did this happen? Why did he do this, especially on my birthday? What did I do to infuriate him so much? Was it my fault? I immediately went to the front desk and checked into a different room, just in case he somehow escaped and tried to find me. I was afraid, but I was also fearful for him. I didn't know what was going to happen to him while he was incarcerated. I had no idea if he was going to spend one night or ten months in custody.

I tried to phone my parents, but they didn't answer. I called my friend Rochelle who lived in Tennessee. I've known her since we were kids. Rochelle talked to me for approximately an hour. I told her Paul strangled me and the cops took him away. She responded, "You need to leave him. You don't deserve this Michelle." I didn't know what to think. Through my sobs, I told her, "He has been really stressed out, I can't just give up on him."

Paul called my cell phone from jail to "talk things out." When Rochelle and I hung up, I answered his call and he said, "I'm sorry and I can't believe how things got so out of control." He eventually persuaded me to drive to jail and bail him out. "Please help me, Michelle. I promise I will never do this again." I tracked down a bail bondsman and started the process of getting Paul released. I went back to the hotel and slept for a few restless hours until he was finally let go. Paul was released around 10 a.m. the next morning. Paul said with tears in his eyes, "I don't know what got into me, Michelle. I love you, I don't ever want to hurt you."

I should have run far, far away, but I didn't. I stayed because he cried, because I loved him, because I put all of my hopes and dreams into him. He apologized over and over. I couldn't admit to myself this was *not* the first time Paul physically hurt me, I didn't allow myself to remember the event outside the nightclub or my head going through the drywall in our bedroom. Later that morning, Paul and I packed up my hotel room and drove to a rodeo in Ventura. Paul held my hand and occasionally cried. He said, "You are my life, Michelle. Nothing like this will ever happen again." I believed him, and told myself, "There's no way he'll do this again."

I was reluctant to talk with anyone in detail about how my situation was worsening. I told my friends and family, "I love Paul so much and we're making a ton of plans for the future." That statement wasn't a lie, it was just lacking pertinent information. I never told them about my birthday. When asked, I responded, "We had a great time." I even told Rochelle, "I am staying with him. He won't hurt me again."

I used my diary as a way to put what was happening to me on paper. A passage from August 20, 2012 read:

"... Let's see, he blames me for "acting like a whore"-just that word, I shouldn't be with him. He thinks I should be ok with him leaving me to go fucking talk to women I don't know, I don't fucking care if they are his friends. He also expects me to stop a fight when i didn't know what was going on??? WTF

He started fucking up right before he bought me a car. He started distancing himself and controlling me. I.E... classes are dumb, why are you going? You are wasting your time running around in circles. You don't need to work... then why the fuck do you throw it in my face? You want to take someone completely out of an environment that she is used to, put her into an unfamiliar situation and expect her to be happy go lucky and wake up with a *sense of purpose? Paul, you took that from me. If you didn't disrespect me, talk about fucking other women, talk down to me, strangle me, always assume that just because you have $ you can buy love, call me whore, slut, use the word cunt in my presence, tell me what to do without a please or thank you, call me stupid idiot, don't trust me because you don't want me talking to anyone.*

Expect me to apologize- 1st when your fucking damn anger problem prevents you from showing love when I need it, not just when its convenient for you. Yell at me, throw everything you get me in my face- which makes me not want anything from you EVER. Then maybe I could wake up happy and wanting to do something with my life. FUCK YOU!"

Paul occasionally came home in an amazing mood and would pick me up and twirl me around the living room. He'd look into my eyes and tell me, "I care about you so much, I love you, Michelle." Although he was abrupt and short with me most of the time, I granted him many second and third chances. When I was upset, I wrote in my diary what I wanted to tell Paul, but the words never escaped my lips. I used the diary as an outlet.

I eventually reached out to a mutual friend about what happened on my birthday. Jessica was a school teacher who helped many kids overcome their violent pasts. She was about forty-five years old, short, and had brunette hair. I thought she might be able to guide me since she had known Paul since he was a child. She warned me, "He will hurt you again and next time it could be worse." Jessica was very knowledgeable, and she continued advising me on ways to prevent a future attack.

Jessica and I met secretly behind the local Kmart to share a cigarette and discuss Paul a few times a week. She had witnessed Paul's rage as a teenager and though she was never physically hurt by him, she recognized some of the characteristics he possessed of being an abuser, both psychologically and physically. "Paul is a narcissist," she said. "He won't ever take responsibility for his actions or admit his wrongdoings." She told me he would always blame me for triggering him and causing fights. Jessica advised me, "Always carry your ID and a credit card on you just in case Paul snaps." I had to hide a single credit card and my ID in my bra or boots when Paul and I went out. Paul always said he wanted to take care of me and he didn't understand why I had to bring anything with me when we went out. It was another form of control and manipulation. I honestly thought Jessica was paranoid, but I listened to what she suggested. I constantly told her, "But I love him...he will never do anything again." Jessica didn't agree.

I went on frequent, long drives to find quiet refuge while Paul was at the office. I'd park and sit under a tree, overlooking the turbulent ocean. The smell of seaweed and salt in the air calmed my nerves. I spoke to God in this stillness, asking Him to change Paul. I never thought to ask God to open my eyes and change me.

My research from the California Attorney General, United States Department of Justice, and The Women's Resource Center helps to illustrate the seriousness of family violence in our nation, violence I was beginning to accept as normal. Here is a combination of results from my research online:

* *One in four murders nationwide involves family relationships.*
* *In California, one in two female homicide victims is murdered by her spouse.*
* *Half of the nation's couples have already had at least one violent incident.*
* *Sixty-three percent of boys ages eleven to twenty who commit homicide, kill the man who is beating their mother.*
* *One out of four high school dating relationships is violent.*
* *Violence is a common occurrence in ten to twenty-five percent of all marriages in the United States.*
* *In half of spouse-abusing families, the children are battered as well.*
* *Abuse-related absenteeism results in an estimated economic loss*

to the country of $3 billion to $5 billion per year, plus another $100 million in medical expenses.
* Five percent of the victims of spousal violence are male.
* Twenty-five percent of all women who are beaten are pregnant.
* Seventy percent of all assault cases involve spousal abuse.

Jessica recommended that I see a local therapist whom she spoke with many times. I started to see Dr. Sandy on August 27, 2012. Paul thought I was going for reasons other than physical and emotional abuse from him. He said, "I'm glad you are going to figure out why you are so insecure and constantly trigger me." Sandy helped me put a lot into perspective, like the fact that the abuse was not my fault. The following are some notes I took during our first meeting:

-He won't let you work, but when he is out of state working, he won't let you leave to see old friends in L.A .(there was a time when he went to the East Coast on a business trip and I wanted to drive to L.A. to see a friend; he wouldn't allow it).
-I need to communicate, but he is constantly on his phone so he never listens to what I had to say.
-I made him more of a priority than myself. I moved to a foreign town and gave up my dreams
-I can do anything. I just need to figure out what I want .
-I need to take time to think about my own life, live for me, not for him.
-Is all this worth it?

I explained to Dr. Sandy that I was tired all the time. She told me, "Being a victim in an abusive relationship requires an exorbitant amount of energy to stay on the abuser's good side." No wonder why I was so exhausted! I made sure Paul had everything he needed or asked for. She also said, "Women tend to make sure everything is in order so they don't upset their abuser in any way."

Paul told me he wanted to go on a trip. Paul said, "Let's go to Playa Del Carmen, Mexico." He thought we should set a date for mid-September and wanted me to plan it, only under his direction and guidance. "I want to take my business partners and your parents on a mind-blowing vacation," he said. Paul told me how to handle the travel agent and gave me detailed instructions for his business partner's and my parents' itinerary. "Make sure my business partners travel first class without any layovers. I want to impress them." I began planning.

A few days before we were scheduled to leave, Paul and I got into an argument on our way home from a convenience store. I don't remember the exact reason the fight started, but I remember being terrified of him. He parked the car in our garage and began shouting at me. "Do you know what it takes for us to go on vacation, Michelle. I've been working all damn year for this and you aren't going to ruin it!" I thought I was doing a great job booking the trip and activities, but not in Paul's mind.

"You are incompetent and going to make me look like an idiot in front of Ronald and Jackie!" I liked Ronald, his primary business partner, very much. I also liked his wife, Jackie. She was three inches taller than Ronald, stick thin and had a sophisticated demeanor. I told Paul, "I talked to Jackie a lot about what they wanted to do, and they seem excited." Paul just answered, "You better not fuck this up."

Usually Paul was drinking when he scolded me that bad, this was the first time he reprimanded me without being intoxicated. I said to him, "I don't want to go to Mexico with you anymore; you scare me, Paul!" He punched the passenger side window, just inches from my head, and said, "If you cancel your trip and make me look stupid, you will have to watch your back." I was fearful of what that meant and decided to travel with him, put a smile on my face, and pretend everything was peachy-keen.

I was delusional and thought maybe going to Mexico would be the saving grace of our tumultuous relationship. If I was going to be forced to go on vacation with Paul then I should think positively and enjoy myself, I thought. The illusion I imagined was falling in love all over again while watching a picturesque sunset on the beaches of Playa Del Carmen.

It was either day three or day four of our vacation in Mexico when Paul drank too much.

"If you try to leave this hotel room, you will have to keep one eye open at all times. If you leave and make me look like an idiot, you will regret it for the rest of your life."

He assaulted me, both verbally and physically. He strangled me and forced me to stay in our hotel room, standing in front of the doorway if I tried to run. I yelled, "You are an idiot, Paul," which caused his temper to escalate. He lurched toward me, pushed me down and strangled me while screaming at me and spitting in my face. If I made any attempt to go towards the door or the sliding glass patio Paul stood in my way and pushed me to the ground. The next morning he apologized as usual saying, "I'm so sorry, Michelle, I won't do it again."

On day seven, Ronald and Jackie left and my parents arrived. I put a smile on my face so my mom and dad wouldn't think anything was wrong. I'm super close to my family and purposefully kept them in the dark- which was very difficult. My parents stayed in a suite I arranged for them for one week. I can do this, I thought. I can pretend.

We went to dinner, spent many hours by the pool, and went parasailing. This was one of my favorite activities during the trip. My mom squealed like a little girl fifty feet in the air. "Oh my God," she yelled. Paul and my dad hit it off and watched sports together in the bar. The views were amazing, the rooms were magnificent and I couldn't tell them the week before I was violently forced into staying in Mexico. I couldn't tell them the strapping, handsome, young man that just paid for their vacation was abusing their baby girl.

Mexico was a joke. If I had gone to this amazing country with anyone else, it probably would have been the best vacation of my life. Instead it was pretty turbulent. Paul didn't get physically abusive with me again on our trip, but he was just an ass. I stayed on my best behavior, making sure to look behind my back and kept track of how many cocktails Paul had. He typically physically hurt me when he had too much to drink, so I paid close attention. When I thought he was drinking too heavily, I said something. "Paul, I think you've had enough. You don't want to hurt me again, do you?"

The trip wasn't all bad. In Mexico, I swam with turtles and dolphins, went zip lining, and ate at really great restaurants. The last week of our stay in Playa, we rented the penthouse suite. The room had its own sparkling private pool on the roof. I was able to sunbath naked without anyone noticing. One night Paul was in an amazing mood. We ate fish for dinner, drank dry Tempranillo wine, and went back to our penthouse. Paul made love to me in our rooftop pool while it was pouring down sheets of rain on us. He occasionally stopped and said, "You look amazing tonight, Michelle. I love you."

Once we got back to the U.S., things continued as normal, except we got a dog. Paul said, "It's a good idea for you to have something to take care of, Michelle." I had enough to take care of, but he couldn't be discouraged. We picked up a terrier/chihuahua mix at a truck stop on the way to Bakersfield for a meeting on September 29, 2012. I remember he peed on me twice during our ride, but he was the cutest little thing. He was white and brown with floppy ears. He was tiny, about the size of my forearm. We named him Dodger.

The cycle of abuse didn't stop because we added to our family, though. I tiptoed around Paul, then he'd snap, yell, and scream. Then he would apologize and take me shopping the next day.

According to *The Domestic Violence Sourcebook*, Dr. Lenore Walker found that in about two-thirds of violent homes, there are three phases the couple goes through over and over, in a circular pattern. First the tension building stage, when the man becomes irritable, edgy and critical of the woman. A woman may go out of her way to keep the peace. She avoids anything that may trigger or irritate him. She tries to pacify him. He gradually becomes more abusive, typically with "minor" incidents such as verbal abuse, increased controlling techniques, or slapping. The woman stays docile hoping that the abuse doesn't escalate. However, the docile behavior legitimizes his belief that he is all-powerful and has a right to be abusive. This very uncomfortable stage in the relationship can last a period of a few days to a few years. Many women feel as if the psychological torture of this stage is the worst.

Then comes the second stage which is the violent outburst with acute battering. Usually the man will become enraged and violent for no apparent reason, or a stated reason that seems petty or irrational, such as Paul's "buyer's remorse." Anything can be the catalyst for the explosion, even if it was not of the woman's doing. An extremely bad day at work, or someone cutting him off on the freeway, for example. The man flies into a destructive rampage. Men in this stage are extremely irrational.

After the extreme violence and the brutality comes the loving contrition. This third phase is a period of great relief for both parties. He has let go of tension and she doesn't have to "walk on eggshells." The man is remorseful and apologetic. He is non-violent and may beg for forgiveness and go out of his way to be kind. Paul always took me to dinner, the movies and shopping. He promised that he would never hurt me again. He was especially apologetic after really brutal fights. "Michelle, I don't think I can live without you," he'd say. He then would spend thousands of dollars on me to ensure that I wouldn't leave him, that I was up for the challenges that arose.

A victim often believes every word, every sentiment during this stage. She thinks that his promises are real and true and that he won't hurt her again. She sees what appears to be an ideal and loving relationship between two healthy individuals. The last stage in this cycle clearly identifies why women end up stuck in an abusive relationship. Her love is real for him, and especially during this phase, his love is real for her. Many women believe they are the sole source of the man's emotional support and feel that it is her responsibility for his temperament and well-being. Dr. Walker believes this phase may be the most psychologically victimizing because it perpetuates the illusion of interdependence. He depends on her for forgiveness and she depends on the "real" man coming back.

This is an outline I found online from the California Judicial System, further explaining the cycle of domestic violence.

Cycle of Domestic Violence

Domestic violence often becomes a pattern made up of three stages

1. *Tension-building phase;*
   a. Batterer-may: pick fights; act jealous; be critical; yell; swear; use angry gestures; coercion; threats; be moody; unpredictable; and drink or use drugs
   b. Partner-may: feel like they are walking gone egg shells; afraid; anxious; try to reason; act calm; appease the batterer or keep silent, and try to keep children quiet.
2. *Violence-crisis phase;*
   a. Batterer-may: verbally, emotionally or physically abuse; sexually assault; restrain or threaten partner and destroy property.
   b. Partner-may: experience fear; shock; use self-defense; try to leave; call for help; pray for it to stop; do what is necessary to survive.

3. Seduction-calm phase;

a. Batterer-may: apologize; minimize or deny abuse; ask for forgiveness; be affectionate; promise it won't happen again and to change; give gifts (this also explains how three dynamics-love, hope, and fear, keep the cycle in motion and make it hard to end a violent relationship)*

b. Partner-may: forgive; feel hopeful; manipulated; blame self; arrange for counseling; return home, and minimize of deny abuse.

Graph of The Cycle of Domestic Violence

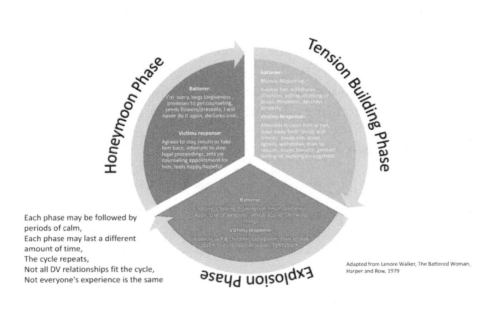

Each phase may be followed by periods of calm,
Each phase may last a different amount of time,
The cycle repeats,
Not all DV relationships fit the cycle,
Not everyone's experience is the same

Adapted from Lenore Walker, The Battered Woman, Harper and Row, 1979

Chapter Seven: Halloween

October 2012

In October, the second stage of the cycle of domestic violence came to a head in our relationship. Paul and I decided to meet a few of his friends at a Halloween party held at a local hotel. I enjoyed going out to parties, dressing up, and meeting people, but because of Paul's schedule we rarely went out. I hated being stuck in the house with him all alone if he was grumpy or agitated, which was frequent because of the stress he had from work. I got stir crazy doing the same thing over and over; wake up, get Paul ready for work, clean up the house, go for a hike, run errands for him, come home, make dinner, then watch a movie, and go to sleep. I was ready for a change and excited for a party!

We arrived at the event and bought drink tickets. Paul was not in the Halloween spirit so neither of us were in costumes, but there were others dressed like fairy godmothers, sex kittens, and zombies. People were fawning and groping one another on the dance floor. Paul's friend Jeff and his girlfriend Samantha met us for the night. Jeff was tall with dark hair and had a mischievous grin. His girlfriend Samantha was a personal trainer with a rock solid body. "The Electric Slide" started to play and I immediately wanted to dance. I pulled Paul, Jeff, and Samantha to the floor. "C'mon guys, it's gonna be so much fun," I said. By the end of the song, we were all laughing and making fun of the silly costumes and dance moves.

Paul bought more drink tickets, and by the end of the night we were all pretty intoxicated. We danced and watched various people make fools of themselves, witnessing a group of women in their fifties hustling a group of twenty-one-year-old boys. I overheard one woman say to her conquest, "I will give you the time of your life." I laughed out loud. Watching the interaction between them was absolutely hilarious. I noticed a few of the boys accepted room keys from the women, and I could only imagine what went on upstairs.

When the promoters closed the event, Paul said, "Let's stay at the hotel with Jeff and Samantha." I thought it was a great idea because we were both too drunk to drive. Jeff said, "It's totally cool if you guys want to crash." Jeff and Samantha thought beforehand and intelligently reserved a room. Samantha passed out, so we let her sleep while we went to the roof with a bunch of people. The crowd gave us drinks and we mingled and laughed with our new acquaintances.

Paul noticed a group of guys were in close proximity to me and he thought I was flirting with them. Paul questioned, "What the hell are you doing, Michelle?" He became very angry, started pushing me, and told me, "It's time to go home." I told him repeatedly, "Why do you think I was flirting, I wasn't!" The same old unrealistic delusions took over his senses. "I saw you," he said. "I know what you were doing." He grabbed me by the arm and took me downstairs to get our things from the hotel room.

"Bro, you two should stay here, you're pretty drunk," Jeff said. He was confused as why Paul suddenly decided to leave, but he let Paul take me to the car. We stumbled down the cold, cement hotel steps that led to the gravel parking lot. We reached the car and he unlocked the doors. Paul was black out drunk and slurring his speech. He screamed at me about the imagined situation. He yelled, "Get in the fucking car, Michelle." I obliged. I was fearful of him driving drunk, but I was more fearful of what he would do to me if I didn't listen. He got in the driver's seat and we were off, speeding down the freeway, swerving in and out of traffic, all the way home.

When we arrived at the house he was belligerent with me. He walked around to the passenger side of the car and heaved the door open, almost ripping off the handle. He pulled me out of the car and forcefully dragged me to the front door of our house. The house was left unlocked because he hated fumbling with keys. He swung open the right side of the white double doors and pushed me through the entry way, staggering in, slamming the door, and locking it behind him. He started breaking things in the house and screaming at me at the top of his lungs. "Who the hell do you think you are?" he asked. He kicked holes in the drywall in the entry way, the kitchen, and the living room. He grabbed knickknacks around the house and threw them against the walls, decimating them to pieces.

I pleaded with him, "I didn't do anything wrong." I told him that his thoughts were inaccurate and he should have more faith in me. Through my sobs, I said, "I was enjoying the party, just like you, and you freaked out for no reason!" I tried to console him, appease him, and pacify him. I said, "You're the love of my life, I want to spend the rest of my life with you, I didn't flirt with those guys." Paul wouldn't believe it.

He tore pictures off the wall in the study and slammed them on the hardwood floors. I was sitting on our little brown suede love seat in the study area when he grabbed the overarching floor lamp from behind the settee. He ripped the cord right out of the wall and it came very close to hitting me in the head. I crouched to avoid the devastation.

I cried, losing my breath and gasping for air in between sobs. I begged him, "Stop destroying our home." I asked him to stop screaming at me and to calm down. Paul grabbed me from the sofa and pulled me into our bedroom. He threw me on the bed and put his strong hands around my throat and applied so much force on my trachea that I couldn't breathe.

I struggled to break free from his grip and rolled off the bed to our bedroom floor. With his strength, he removed the mirror off of our cherrywood vanity dresser and threw it over my head. At this point, I got on my knees and begged God, "Please forgive him, he doesn't know what he's doing." With his devilish smirk, Paul laughed and replied, "God isn't going to help you now."

I was terrified. I thought that Paul was going to kill me. The smirk on his face was demonic. I started to tremble and began thinking of different ways to keep myself alive, to postpone my imminent death. I tried to run from him. I sprang forward toward the locked front door, but he deflected me.

I finally made it out of the house after skillfully navigating around his advances in my direction. I ran. I ran as hard and as fast as I could. I made it halfway down the block and heard his breath panting behind me. I ran faster and harder. I lost my sandals and could feel the cool cement of the sidewalk beneath my feet.

He caught up with me. Paul was taller and his adrenaline fueled his speed. He grabbed me by my long, blonde hair and pulled me to the ground. I screamed. Paul then kicked me and said, "Shut the hell up and get back to the house before someone sees what you're doing, Michelle." He blamed me! He accused me of causing this fight that was happening on our friendly neighborhood block. He promised, "I'll stop and we can talk this out when we get back to the house." I followed his instructions. I felt like I was trapped. I didn't have any other options. With his left hand around the back of my neck, Paul steered me towards our house. I was crying hysterically and begged him, "Don't hurt me anymore."

When we reached our home, the front door was wide open. Paul, in his frenzy, had stormed out of the house, running after me, without any awareness of his surroundings. He shoved me into the entry way and slammed the door behind him. I turned around from where I was and looked at him helplessly while he panted like a dog. I couldn't see any blue in his eyes. His pupils were completely dilated, covering his irises entirely, leaving only black holes staring back at me. I hardly recognized the man standing in front of me. Paul was completely out of control, unrestrained and overtaken by some force that I could not identify.

He started yelling at me again. I told him, "You're right, I shouldn't have flirted with those guys, I'm sorry." I thought if I told Paul what he wanted to hear, it might prevent him from coming after me again. It didn't. My agreeable attitude infuriated him even more. He lurched forward and took me by my throat.

Our bedroom was immediately off to the right side of the entry way. He forced me into the bedroom and threw me on the bed. He strangled me until I almost passed out. I remember I couldn't take a breath and I felt like I was suffocating. He let go of my throat only to let me take in oxygen for a short while before grabbing me again.

Paul's favorite way to keep me quiet was to put his fingers under my tongue and press down as hard as he could to draw blood. While obstructing my mouth, he would take his other hand and put it around my throat to constrict air flow while he pushed me on the bed. He never punched me in the face, but he applied so much pressure on the right side of my face that it swelled like I was a boxer finishing a brutal twelve-round match.

He lifted my helpless body up from the bed and made me stand. Then he threw me into our closet on top of a metal three-tier shoe rack that collapsed upon impact. I fell onto it with the right side of my body. It hurt, and I knew I was going to bruise. Paul screamed at me, "Get up." I barely had the energy to beg him to stop. He grabbed me and threw me against a wall in our bathroom, leaving a hole in the drywall where my head hit. This time it went all the way through the wall.

"Paul, please stop" I shouted. He didn't listen. I was powerless and defenseless against him.

He continued his onslaught. Paul spit in my face and I collapsed to the ground. I wiped the saliva from my face and felt his piercing glare through my soul. He came at me again and again and again.

This incident lasted roughly four hours. When he finally started to sober up, he became aware of what he was doing. By this time, I was bloodied, bruised, and exhausted from the beating. He took me into the shower with him, I was so paralyzed by the events of the evening that I didn't have the energy to lift my arms. He washed my hair and washed the blood out of my mouth and off of my body.

I recall him trying to soothe me by saying, "Everything will be alright. I love you Michelle." I thought that maybe this was true. He held me up in the shower because my body was too weak to stand. His words were just sounds in the background along with the water cascading from the shower head on my brittle body. I was dazed and almost incoherent. He tried talking to me, but I couldn't keep focus. I couldn't believe what happened.

I didn't even try to comb through my wet, straggly hair. The knots were countless and clumps of hair were coming out in handfuls. I laid down soaking wet on our bed, feeling like a drowned rat that barely survived a storm in a New York City gutter. He laid down next to me and held my hand, possibly thinking that would keep me from escaping. I couldn't even dream of an exit strategy; I was too sore and debilitated to move. I prayed for death, but instead I drifted in and out of consciousness.

The next morning when I woke up, Paul was staring at me. As soon as I opened my eyes, he immediately began to cry. My face looked like it was used as a human punching bag. I had a black eye like no other black eye I had ever seen. You couldn't see any white in my eye and everything was scarlet red, I was fortunate my vision wasn't obstructed by the blood.

Paul wouldn't allow me to go to the hospital. He said, "Your injuries look like domestic violence and I don't want the hospital calling the police." I wish I would have found the strength to go to the police, or at least get checked out by a physician at the local E.R, but I didn't. He said, "What happened to you isn't domestic violence. I just got triggered and lost control, I won't do it again."

Paul apologized to me every hour for the first few days. He held me and cried with me, making me believe he wouldn't hurt me again. Paul soothed my sobs with words of affirmation, "You're beautiful, you deserve so much in life and we can create that together." He said that he made a huge mistake and he was sorry. In another breath he told me, "Your face isn't that bad. Don't panic, it will heal."

I knew this was wrong, I knew that this was not the fairy tale that I desired. I was too frightened to argue with Paul about what happened, too frightened to attempt to leave. I thought that nothing could be as bad as this beating and believed that Paul wouldn't hurt me again. He learned his lesson, I thought, and perhaps we could move forward without any more violence.

I didn't have the courage to look at myself in a mirror until a couple days after this horrific event. While Paul was working, I looked in the mirror at my swollen face and didn't even recognize myself. I began to cry while touching the unhealed wounds. My lips were cracked, my cheeks swollen, and my eye was filled with a cream-colored crusty discharge. Paul kept a baseball bat beside our bed in case of robbers and I took the metal bat and swung it at the mirror in the guest bathroom. The mirror broke and I swung again and again. It shattered all over the floor, stretching into the hallway outside. I dropped the bat and went into the living room and fell on the couch. The salty tears streaming down my face stung. "I have to calm myself down," I said aloud.

I was in utter shock. I didn't know what to do. I felt my soul reaching for answers, reaching for a reason why I deserved this. I wanted to call the police, I wanted justice, but I was so scared and torn between love and proceeding with prosecution. I understood that this was wrong, I just didn't understand how wrong. I wanted our relationship to work so badly. I needed it to work.

Paul came home and found me lying on the couch. He noticed the glass in the hallway and walked into the guest bathroom. He yelled at me for breaking the mirror. He took me by my shoulders and shook me. "What the hell is wrong with you, Michelle?" he said. I didn't answer, I just glared at him. He cleaned up the mess while I stayed on the couch staring at the ceiling. He then covered every mirror in the house with fabric so I wouldn't look at my face.

I am not sure what was going on in Paul's head. My face looked awful, I'm sure he felt some real remorse, but maybe not. His treatment of me was very bi-polar at this time. He would apologize and in the next sentence he would brush it off saying "It's not as bad as you think." This must've made him feel better, perhaps like his abuse was acceptable.

I was in a lot of pain for several weeks after this incident. I was trying to numb the pain with alcohol and expired prescription pain pills I found in random drawers around the house. Nothing seemed to work. Paul hated drugs, but he hated me whining about the pain even more. He suggested, "Call my brother to get marijuana and see if that helps." I did, and it worked. This was the only time Paul allowed me to smoke weed, to dull the agony and alleviate my discomfort.

My eye stayed a dim yellow for about eight months after the attack. Many people asked me if I had jaundice. One of Paul's employees asked me, "Why do you always seem to have bruises, wear long-sleeves and wear sunglasses?" I laughed and told her, "I like to hike and I fall down a lot."

A piece of glass remained in my left thumb for five years from this altercation. In Paul's rampage, he broke the lamp above the bed and fragments of the incandescent light bulb fell all over our mattress. In the course of him throwing me on the bed and me fighting to break free, a small sliver of the bulb went underneath my thumb nail. Approximately eight months later, I saw a doctor to get the glass removed. However, the minor operation was unsuccessful. I mainly felt the piercing stab of the glass when I put on sneakers or used my left hand to open a jar. It finally protruded out in 2018.

I can't tell you why I stayed after this horrendous catastrophe. I honestly thought Paul would change. I excused his behavior because I believed it was the alcohol impairing his judgement. In the book *Domestic Violence: Opposing Viewpoints*, it reads, "Studies have shown that though domestic violence is universal, it is more prevalent in substance abusers. F. Hilberman and M. Munson found that 93 percent of the persons causing violence on their wives were alcoholics. Marvin E. Wolfgang reported that in his study, 67 percent of husbands who beat their wives were alcoholics."

The common denominator is that domestic violence is higher among substance abusers. Domestic violence could be significantly dwindled if we could reduce drug and alcohol addiction among men, women and teens, in my opinion. I also do not believe that it is the only cause of domestic violence. There have been many studies done where the abuser and the victim have had no alcohol in their systems. I think that if an abuser chooses to lose control and attacks their loved ones, it is a conscious choice deep within them and if they wanted to, they could control it. I don't think Paul cared enough to quit drinking.

The following photographs are of my face once I could gain the strength to look in the mirror. I took these pictures approximately two days after this beating. I thought that by including these pictures they could accurately describe what happened that horrible day in October.

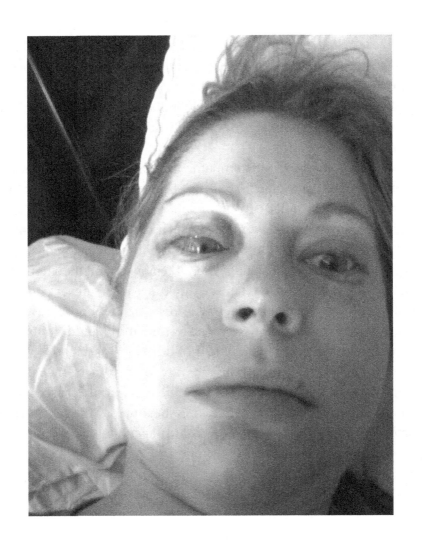

Chapter Eight: A Holiday From Hell

December 2012

I accepted Paul's apology for the beating in October. I continued making excuses for his behavior the duration of our relationship. It's hard to look back and describe my feelings during this time. I remember thinking he was the best I could do. Paul loved me and supported me, I thought. He caused me harm, but there were times of wonder and awe. Times that I would look into his eyes and see his tender aching soul. Times where we would hold each other while he opened up to me about his hardships. "My life hasn't been easy, Michelle..." The hardships encompassed my very being and made me have sympathy for him. Because of this sympathy, I stayed thinking I could help fix him.

There was one time in the course of my healing that Paul took me out to dinner on the pier for a romantic dinner by the ocean. I wore my sunglasses in the restaurant and Paul and I took a table in the back corner. The waitress asked us, "What can I get you to drink?" I ordered a glass of wine and she asked me for my ID to make sure I was of age. I handed her my driver's license and she kindly said, "Can you please take off your sunglasses?" I was reluctant, but I knew I had to remove the glasses if I wanted a cocktail. I took them off, and felt her narrow gaze at my eye and swollen cheeks. She immediately apologized and said she would be right back with my wine. I was utterly humiliated and exhausted from keeping secrets.

I was overwhelmed with Paul's demands and psychological abuse. I had no energy left for anything. The only physical activity that was consistent in my life was hiking. I would hike to meditate and talk with God. Well, actually, to *yell* at God. I did a lot of screaming and cursing at Him in the middle of a mountain with nothing but nature surrounding me.

"Why is Paul like this, God? Why can't You fix him?" I'd see animals scurrying and hear birds chirping. Most of the time, it was warm without a cloud in the sky, the warmth of the sun permeating my skin. I'd feel God bring me to Matthew 18:21-22: *"Then Peter came up and said to him, 'Lord, how often will my brother sin against me, and I forgive him? As many as seven times?' Jesus said to him, 'I do not say to you seven times, but seventy-seven times."*

I thought this verse meant I should stay with Paul. I have now realized that forgiving someone does not mean to stay in an unhealthy situation; it simply means to forgive so you don't hold onto resentment, detestation and hate. I misunderstood what God was saying and I didn't leave an abusive environment when I should have.

It took me about four weeks to heal from all the bruises except for my eye. I barely went outside during this time, and when I did I would wear a ball cap and dark sunglasses. I was embarrassed. I thought the reason I got beat was because of something I did wrong.

After I healed, Paul and I went to one of my favorite restaurants where I had a melt-in-your-mouth filet mignon with crumbled blue cheese and Laetitia Pinot Noir. After dinner, Paul drove us home, and sure enough, we got into some argument about something petty in the car. When we arrived home Paul said, "I'm going for a walk." He chose to walk outside instead of physically assaulting me.

I was frustrated and felt powerless. I looked for any way to numb the emotional pain I was in. While Paul was walking, I took a dull razor blade from Paul's tool box, pressed it on the skin of the inside of my right ankle, and drug it through my skin for two inches. I didn't want to kill myself, just to make something else hurt instead of my heart. After I cut my ankle, I kicked a hole in the wall in the dining room with my Steve Madden black stilettos, and put a Band-Aid on my wound.

Paul didn't react to the hole in the wall when he came back. He was so consumed in his own world that he didn't notice it. There were dents and holes all over from Paul's explosions and he must've assumed it had been there the whole time. "Let's go to bed," is all he said.

Paul and I were in the "walking on eggshells" part of the cycle of domestic violence now. I was trying to make sure I didn't upset him in any way, to avoid a physical altercation. There was a buildup of emotions. He was super grouchy one minute then wanting to have sex the next. My head was spinning with his mood swings.

During Christmas, Paul came to Idaho to visit my family with me. We didn't fly into my mom and dad's town. We actually flew to Umatilla, Oregon first so we could visit my brother Josh, who was in prison at the time. Josh was arrested for possession of meth and robbery of a pharmacy.

We thought we had gotten Paul approved for a visit but to our surprise, he couldn't get into the facility because of the incident during my birthday when the police were involved. I visited Josh by myself and told my brother, "Paul isn't able to come because he has an important phone call. He said he'd make sure to come next time." Josh didn't mind. It gave us longer to catch up, although I left out important details about my life. After our visit, Paul and I made the five-hour drive to Sandpoint, Idaho in a rental car to my parents' house.

It started to snow. Not just white, flaky, soft snow, but a blizzard. I drove because I knew where I was going and didn't trust Paul's driving in winter, with good reason. Paul grew up in California and never experienced extreme weather conditions. Paul was freaking out to say the least. Every few minutes he would tell me, "You're driving too fast and not paying enough attention to the road."

He was lecturing me in the middle of a snowstorm when all my attention needed to be on the road. After all of Paul's pathetic attempts to distract me, I finally looked at him and sternly said, "Shut the fuck up." He actually listened and we continued our drive north for another four hours. By the time we reached Spokane, cars were pulled over on the side of the road, big semis were stopped in the middle of the freeway, and we saw cars flipped over in the ditch on the side of the highway. We arrived at my parents unharmed, except for my spirit, which Paul seemed to crush in the first two hours of the drive.

The night before Christmas, my family threw our annual dinner party with a few friends and all of our relatives. My dad, Paul, and I went to the mountain to ski and snowboard before the party began. We went down the backside of the mountain, my dad's favorite side. It was ice-packed with a fresh layer of white powder. My dad said, "I'll race you down." Paul and I geared up to go. Halfway down, the California boy took a nasty tumble, knocked his pretty little head on the ground, and began to throw a tantrum, tossing his board in the snow. Paul said, "Let's leave," so my dad and I packed up our things and drove back to the house.

Paul had a headache from the fall and laid down in my room when we got home. I let him rest while I went into the living room to mingle with my family. A few hours later, Paul emerged from the bedroom and began drinking…a lot. Once again, it was his favorite, Vodka Red Bull. He could easily put down four drinks in the matter of a half hour and he got buzzed.

My parents and my uncle went into the master bedroom and locked the door behind them to chat. Paul spoke to me sternly before we arrived at my parents' house, saying, "No one is allowed to use drugs while I'm visiting!" Paul knew nothing for sure, but he assumed they were doing cocaine in that locked bedroom. He blew up at me, screaming, "I shouldn't have come to this fucking town." He told me what horrible human beings my parents were to act like this in his presence.

I had a few cocktails and didn't know how to combat his derogatory comments about my family. I said, "They are just talking," but that didn't mollify his temper. I felt as if I were stuck in the middle of a rock and a hard place. Paul started to pack his things and attempted to call a cab to drive him to the Spokane Airport, on Christmas Eve, in the middle of a snowstorm, in Sandpoint, Idaho. He was unsuccessful, of course. My dad, hearing the commotion, came out of the room and went into the garage with Paul to try and deflate the situation. My dad told Paul, "Calm down, buddy, and get some sleep. Nothing can be done right now."

Paul eventually came to bed, but left my family with a sour taste in their mouth. Paul did some ass kissing the next couple of days. He accompanied my dad and me to a local ski and snowboard store the day after Christmas. Paul said to my dad, "I want to buy you new ski boots to apologize for the other night." Paul bought my dad a pair of expensive, heat-molding boots that were supposed to be comfortable on my dad's swelling calf and foot due to his diagnosis of Intervene Thrombosis. He bought my dad a pair of skis and poles to match along with a winter coat, hat, and goggles.

My father was not one to fall for bribes, but Paul was super charming. He succeeded in buying back my dad's approval. Dad said, "It seems like Paul is taking care of you, Michelle. That's what's important." I laughed and said, "Okay, Dad."

My mom on the other hand was very suspicious. My mom couldn't be bought. She gazed at Paul most nights while we sat on the couch watching the Western Digital Television that Paul purchased them. Her hands were crossed and her eyes squinted at Paul. My mom suspected something was wrong and told me, "I'm not sure if I like him."

After staying at my parents for approximately a week and a half, Paul and I flew home to make it to a party on New Year's Eve. On December 31, Paul and I went to a local club hosting a celebration for New Years. We went with Paul's friend Jeff, Samantha, his brother, and sister-in-law. Paul's brother Jack, was awesome. He was very good looking, had blondish hair, chewed tobacco, and wore cowboy boots most everywhere. Jack's wife Nicole, was a bit naive, wore glasses, and rarely smiled.

Nicole dragged me to the dance floor and after five or so songs, she asked me, "Let's go outside to cool off, I need some fresh air." When I came back in from the patio, I found Paul on the dance floor, glaring at me with accusatory eyes. He took his full glass of liquor and poured it on my head, causing liquid to puddle under my feet. The look of hell entered his face. His eyes became black, overwhelmingly so that you could not see any of his beautiful blue irises.

I had no idea what was to come, I just felt chills go up my spine. His look scared the shit out of me. After what happened in October, I didn't think he would assault me again, but I intuitively knew something was very wrong.

Paul suddenly grabbed my arm with the intention of dragging me outside. A male patron intervened by stepping in front of Paul and demanded, "Let her go." Paul hit him in the face and broke his nose. Blood flowed from the stranger's face onto his clothing and on the dance floor. I eventually broke free of Paul's grip, and ran for fear to the restroom with Nicole in tow. Nicole repeatedly assured me Paul wasn't going to do anything to harm me physically. She was ignorant of the fact that Paul brutally beat me just two months earlier. I came out of the bathroom and questioned Paul, "Why are you so angry with me?" He said, "You were secretly trying to have sex with a man outside!" It was Paul's delirious thoughts that ran his life when he was drinking; his insane, manic, and hallucinatory nature controlled him.

Paul and I walked outside towards the valet with our friends following close behind. Once we reached the end of the sidewalk, Paul lurched towards me. He grabbed my throat with both of his strong hands, lifted me up by my neck and slammed me down on the cement bench just outside the entryway; the bench meant for lovers to sit and rest while they glimpse the amazing cliff side. My head bounced twice.

Jeff told me later he thought I had died.

There was a large congregation of people present, many of them tried to pull Paul off of me, and many stood in shock watching the event. The valet at the hotel screamed, "I'm calling the police." The next thing I knew, Paul, Jack, and Nicole were nowhere to be found.

Two officers showed up and started asking me questions. I told the police what happened through my tears. One officer asked me if I wanted to press charges. I said, "Yes, this is going to be the last time Paul does this to me." With encouragement from the other officer who knew and despised Paul, I gave my testimony. Jeff sat on the bench watching while I spoke to the police. Samantha was already in their hotel room by the time the police showed up.

I was scared to go home and decided to stay at a hotel. Thank God Jessica advised me to always have a credit card and ID readily available just in case something happened. I put the identification in my bra before Paul and I left the house.

The following statement is from Jeff. I have omitted details about the specific location and names of people involved.

"Dear Sir or Madam:

The following statement is my recollection of and event that occurred on the morning of January 1, 2013 in [], CA:

On December 31, 2012, I visited the [] Restaurant in [], California with Paul and Michelle Jewsbury. We were attending a new Year's Eve party at the restaurant and planned on celebrating the New Year's Holiday at the venue until closing.

Around 12:30-1:00am on January 1st, 2012, approximately 5 hours after I initially arrived at the [], I observed Paul and Michelle arguing at the restaurant bar. The argument quickly became very heated; although I could not hear everything that was said, I could see Paul screaming at Michelle and using very vulgar language toward her. I observed this behavior for approximately

30 seconds, at which time Paul's body language became extremely aggressive, as did his verbal language. The argument escalated into a physical confrontation as Paul poured his drink on Michelle's head and grabbed her by the arm in a violence manner. I was standing about 10-15 feet away when this happened and attempted to negotiate my way through the dense crowd in order to break up the confrontation. Around the same time, I noticed a man grab Paul by the shoulder and say "Hey man, you can't put your hands on a woman like that!" Paul quickly turned around and punched the man in the face. The man did not fight back, as it was clear to me by the man's reaction that the force of Paul's punch stunned him. Once I was able to make my way over to Paul, I told him that he needed to walk outside and "have a civil conversation with his girlfriend". he initially was reluctant to do so, but he did agree to step outside and discuss matters with Michelle in a calmer, more civil manner.

After arriving outside, I left Paul and Michelle to work out their issues in front of the restaurant. I stood about 20-30 feet away and observed the two communicate. The couple argues for about 30 seconds before the discussion again escalated. Paul began to use strong, vulgar language towards Michelle. He started to shout very loud at her; I noticed his body language had become very threatening, as if he was going to hit Michelle. I began to walk towards the couple, but by the time I had taken a step, it was too late. Paul hit Michelle in the face and she fell onto a concert bench. Paul then grabbed Michelle by the collar and slammed her head violently into the concrete bench. The sound of her head hitting the concrete was so loud that I feared that he may have injured Michelle severely. When I reached Paul and Michelle, he had her pinned down on the concrete bench. I rushed to the side of Paul and pushed him off of Michelle and told him to leave her alone. Instead of walking away, Paul came right back for more. I could tell he meant business; I could see the look or rage in his eyes, and his approach towards Michelle and I was very aggressive. I grabbed Paul by the collar and pushed him as hard as I could. At that point, one of the restaurant managers yelled out that the "cops are on their way." Upon hearing this, Paul stopped, turned around, and ran towards []. The [] Police arrived about a minute later. They did not look for Paul, nor did there appear to be any sign of him on the premises."

Jeff said in his statement that Paul hit me in the face. I don't remember Paul hitting me, but I was very confused and distraught so it definitely could have happened. I do remember my head on the cement bench bouncing twice, realizing Paul was the one slamming it down.

Paul called me the next day sobbing, apologizing for getting out of control. "I'm so sorry, Michelle," he said. I listened to his excuses for his behavior. He sounded frightened and full of compassion. There was a warrant out for his arrest and he was hiding from the police at a hotel nearby. He assured me, "I will never hurt you again." I responded, "I need a break and want to move back to Los Angeles." I was fearful of his reaction, but he said he understood. I thought maybe if I left, he would get the help he needed.

Paul sent me a few text messages apologizing for what happened. Here are those exact texts:

"I'm really really sorry and hope u can be better and that u can forgive me so u will be free from all of me and what's happened. Sorry for being hurt and lonely and lost."

"Sorry to let u down and squish on your dreams and rob u of individualism and self expression. I'm just tired and have lost my care about allot of things so that's why I'm the way I am."

"No matter what... know I love u and loved u and always will love u and you are wonderful. I'm going to have to make some

choices soon that I need to make and those choices may hurt people around me but that's what I feel I need to do."

I felt sad for Paul. I knew he had problems stemming from childhood and he wasn't taking care of them, causing him to react in unconscious and hurtful ways. I thought he was hitting a new low and I desperately wanted to help him.

We were in the third stage of the cycle of domestic violence and Paul was apologetic, accepting, and remorseful for what he did. Paul seemed secure with my decision to move out and he didn't put up a fight. He assured me, "We will stay together and I will work on my issues." He said he realized hurting me was wrong and he needed help. I believed his lies. I believed he was capable of change.

Paul begged me, "Please drop the charges. I will start therapy to figure out why I have so much anger buried within myself." I agreed to not move forward with prosecution as long as he started and continued with therapy. He did everything right to appease me, causing me to be more sympathetic, not giving consideration to my own circumstances.

I moved out the following week, after having multiple, passionate, secret rendezvous with Paul in his hotel room. He was compassionate and held me tight for hours while we laid in the hotel room together. He didn't let me go easily, but he didn't put up a fight. He said, "You are my past, my present, and my future." He caressed my skin and gently kissed me. He told me, "I know that if we can make it through this, we can make it through anything." Paul stayed in his hotel for a few weeks until his hired attorney could get the arrest warrant revoked.

Even without my help, we learned that the District Attorney decided to prosecute the case. According to the book *Opposing Viewpoints,* research shows that approximately 75 percent of batter cases are dismissed due to the lack of victims help. The victim often times requests to dismiss all charges or fails to appear in court. Although I agreed not to press charges, the DA wanted to move forward.

I did everything Paul's lawyer said to do. "Tell Michelle don't talk to the DA, ever." I remained in Los Angeles so the DA couldn't find me, I didn't return any phone calls from the police or the DA, and I always communicated when the DA tried to reach out to me.

I did all this because I believed Paul. I really thought that with therapy he would change and embrace his imperfections. He would take responsibility for all he had done and turn magically into my Prince Charming. I gave Paul every excuse in the book and trusted him even though his track record was abominable.

Paul and I lived in two different cities in California. Although Paul told me he would drive to spend time with me, more times than not, I drove up the beautiful coast to see him. Every time I arrived in town—which was bi-weekly—he was very careful where we went and who we were seen with, just in case the DA found out where I was and wanted to subpoena me.

The book *Opposing Viewpoints* also states, "Each year an estimated two to four million American women will be physically and/or sexually abused by their male partners. An estimated 30 percent to 66 percent of these women will call the police for help." Of those, many will withdraw the complaint; therefore, enabling the abuser to continue the misconduct.

Paul hired the best attorney in town, paid him fifty thousand in cash under the table, and got off without even a slap on the wrist. I met with Paul's attorney once. He was a persnickety, old, gray-haired man who wore glasses. On June 5, 2013 Paul's attorney had me sign a declaration he wrote. He said, "This will keep Paul out of jail." I signed it without even reading it. I perjured myself without realizing the ramifications of signing a document under penalty or purjery.

Because of my cooperation with Paul and his attorney, the DA had to drop the charges. Paul didn't receive any ramifications for his behavior, affirming his deranged belief that he was invincible. Many health professionals believe that if an abuser doesn't serve any consequences for his or her actions, there will be no cause to change, even if the victim thinks they can persuade the batterer otherwise.

Most women are raised to believe that a woman is the primary caretaker of the family. We are taught that "love conquers all" and if we could just love the man enough, we could "save" him and he would inevitably shift his demeanor. I loved Paul for his infectious personality and astounding charisma. Once again, what kept me coming back was I thought I could change him.

Chapter Nine: Go Dodgers

July 2013

Paul spoke to a therapist who Jessica recommended to him. Dr. Matt excelled in many field's including couples counseling and childhood violence. Jessica had a deep appreciation for Dr. Matt's work and thought he might be able to help Paul. I was happy Paul started talking to someone about his past, his resentment and his anger, thinking Dr. Matt could possibly fix him. The first time he spoke to Dr. Matt was January 4, 2013, and according to Paul, they had a great connection. Dr. Matt was located in L.A., so the two of them had conversations over the phone instead of in person, which I thought was strange, but it seemed to work.

I lived in L.A. and Paul stayed up north. We agreed that a long-distance relationship was best until I felt more comfortable. Paul called me often and said, "I am learning so much, thank you for staying by my side." Paul sent me a number of text messages saying how much he loved me and how he couldn't see his life without me. I had an out. I had an opportunity to end it all, but I got sucked back into his lies and manipulation. He seemed warm and kind-hearted.

I saw improvement in his personality and overall demeanor, so I decided to move back in with him in March, just three months after the attack on New Year's. Up until March, he reassured me of his love and consistently told me his conversations with Dr. Matt were helping greatly. I didn't move all my things back in, just half my wardrobe and some miscellaneous items.

Just to be safe, I kept my apartment in L.A. Paul said, "I will take care of your rent in Los Angeles and prove myself to you." I welcomed his commitment to pay my rent. I told him, "I'm not going to make dinner every night and I am gonna look for a part-time job." He disagreed with me working, but accepted me teaching an acting class once a week at a local theater in town. The theater needed me less than ten hours per week so I could continue taking care of Paul's personal and business needs. Paul also bought himself a new vehicle and said, "I don't want to restrict you anymore. You can drive the Lexus whenever you want."

Once I moved back, I noticed Paul was speaking to Dr. Matt a lot less than he told me. Paul said, "I'm too busy to talk to Matt for an hour every week. I have deals to close." Therapy was not his priority; "I'm healing myself by myself, and I don't need help," he said. Unbeknownst to me, he only spoke to Matt once or twice per month. "What we talk about is none of your business," he said to me after asking him how therapy was going. I didn't argue. When Paul told me Dr. Matt suggested he quit drinking and Paul didn't, I should have known I was still in for a very messy ride.

In May of 2013, Paul asked me, "What kind of dog do you want?" I hesitated to answer because we already had a dog that I was taking care of. "We have Dodger, we don't have room for another dog," I replied. Paul insisted I answer him. I reluctantly said, "A Siberian Husky." Paul immediately began looking up pictures of Husky puppies and sending them to me via text while he was at work.

On Mother's Day, Paul took me to a pet store and told me to "pick a pup." The store was full of Husky puppies. In one of the back cages, there was a black and white puppy with floppy ears and steel blue eyes. His paws were huge and he was uncomfortable on his feet. His goofy personality made me laugh. I asked the clerk if I could hold him, and when I did, I fell in love. We named him Steele.

I treated the dogs like my children. I spoiled them and took them everywhere I went. Whenever Paul had a tantrum, I'd lay with the dogs and it was almost like they knew what was happening and tried to comfort me.

On Saturday July 13, 2013, we left the dogs at a kennel and drove to L.A. to watch a Dodgers baseball game. The Dodgers were playing the Colorado Rockies, a team that won their first National League championship in 2007. They were good and we wanted the Dodgers to beat them.

I dressed in skin tight blue pants, a white blouse and matching high heels. Paul and I bought vodka cocktails from the Dodgers VIP lounge on the main level before going to our seats. The game ended with the Dodgers winning 1-0. Paul was drunk and in a good mood. "Let's go party," he said. To celebrate we went to the club on the bottom floor of our hotel on the Sunset Strip in Hollywood. It was a very exclusive two-story bar that had a sparkling pool in the middle of the main room.

Drinks began flowing. Paul enthusiastically said to most everyone we met, "Let me get this round of drinks!" By the end of the night, Paul and I were pretty intoxicated.

When the bar closed, Paul said to me, "I want to take you upstairs and do nasty things to you." I giggled as we made our way to the second floor where our room was located. Once inside our suite, Paul pushed me against the wall in the walkway and began passionately kissing me, pulling my pants to the ground. I moaned, my hands excitedly moved behind his head and I pulled his blond, short hair. Paul's arousal abruptly ended and he walked into the bedroom leaving me standing pant-less in the entryway alone.

I followed him and asked, "Are you alright?" I thought perhaps he started to get the spins from being so drunk. "I'm tired and want to go to bed," he said. He laid down on the bed and turned on the TV. I was confused, but didn't push the issue. I kissed him on his forehead and told him, "I'm gonna go take a cold shower."

Paul could hear the sound of the water running which fueled his anger. He came into the bathroom after I finished undressing and before I entered the shower and yelled, "You are a slut!" He reached for a small coral statue and threw it at my head. I was stunned. I had no idea where his animosity came from. "Paul, what did I do?" I asked.

He came towards me, took me by my throat, and slammed the back of my head on the wall. The sounds of my cries were muffled by the running water. He dragged my naked body to the bedroom where he pushed me on the bed and forced me face down on the white, goose-down comforter. He placed me on all fours and ripped off his belt. I had never been raped before and screamed, "No!" Paul unbuttoned his pants and thrust his fingers inside of me. He asked me, "Is this how you like it, hard and animalistic?"

I screamed as loud as I could. Our room overlooked Sunset Boulevard and I could see and hear people leaving the club on the floor below. No one heard my screeching. I struggled to get out of the position he held me in. I was able to flip to my back and Paul choked me with his left hand while he pressed under my tongue with the fingers of his right hand, drawing blood. "What the hell were you thinking?" he questioned. I tried to bite his fingers, but my defense made him press harder.

I had no idea what he was talking about. Paul continued and shouted, "Don't flirt with other men." His jealousy triggered his rage.

Paul did to me in this hotel room exactly what he did to me that dreadful night in October, just nine months prior. I was spitting up blood because of the wounds in my mouth and I eventually pretended I couldn't breathe, lying on the bed coughing to see if that would make him stop. I essentially played dead. Paul fearfully said, "I'm going to get help," and left the room. He didn't stay gone long enough for me to even lock the door.

I had no idea the extent of what Paul was capable of doing. I experienced brutality from him before, but didn't know how bad it could get. I thought about ways to escape or how to calm him down, but nothing worked. I felt like a sitting duck, unable to defend myself. Paul was so strong. He was approximately sixty pounds heavier than me and worked out daily. His body weight on top of me was overwhelming. I saw the devil in his eyes.

I thought I was going to die.

Paul's brutal attack ended around five in the morning. Paul sat across from the king-sized bed in our hotel room where I laid. "Are you alright, Michelle?" he asked. I just stared at the ceiling. He carried on a conversation about our plans for the next day and asked me if I still wanted to join him. He spoke to me as if the three-hour beating didn't happen. I asked, "Why did you do this?" He tried to make me believe my bloodied mouth, sore body, and aching throat were somehow not of his accord. "You did this Michelle, not me," he answered.

Paul came to me on the bed and held me, murmuring, "Everything is going to be okay." I was petrified of what he was capable of, so I just laid there letting him believe his consolation was working. I eventually drifted to sleep. In my dreams, I imagined ways I could escape, but woke up anxiety stricken and terrified. I never called the police or reported the crime.

The National Coalition Against Domestic Violence estimates up to 90 percent of battered women never report their abuse. Rape is a regular form of abuse in 50 percent of violent relationships. According to WomensLaw.org, "Rape is forced sexual intercourse. Force doesn't always have to be physical force where the perpetrator physically overpowers the victim; force could include psychological coercion (being "talked into it"), threats to cause harm to the person or a loved one if the person doesn't submit to the sexual intercourse, or other circumstances in which the victim feels that there is no other option than to submit to the unwanted sexual activity. Rape can also include situations where the victim may be drunk, drugged, asleep, unconscious, or for any reason unable to consent. Most legal definitions of rape include vaginal, anal or oral penetration by a body part or an object."

For two years after this incident, I denied the fact that Paul raped me. I thought that because he didn't use his penis to penetrate me, it didn't count and wasn't "bad" enough to be considered rape. I was ashamed to think myself a victim of rape. After years of therapy and research, I finally learned that what Paul did to me was rape. When he thrust his fingers inside of me without my consent, that constituted rape, and it was not my fault.

The next day, Paul and I were scheduled to have lunch with my old roommate Deen and his friend Barney. Some of my clothes were covered in saliva and blood from me coughing up the night before. Paul suggested, "Since you didn't bring a different outfit, let's stop at Sports Authority to get you new clothes." I reluctantly bought a new wardrobe and shoes to change into. My cheeks were swollen, my throat was raw, but most of my injuries were on the inside of my mouth and on my body. Paul learned his lesson from the October attack to not leave marks on my face. We arrived at Deen's house just in time to have food. I said, "I don't feel well," and stayed quiet while picking at my lunch.

After lunch, I got in Paul's white Cadillac Escalade, and we drove back home. Paul stopped in Santa Barbara on our way up the coast. He said, "I want to make amends and treat you the way you should be treated." He took me to Nordstrom's, hired a personal shopper, and bought $2,000 worth of clothes and shoes. He thought he could buy my forgiveness, which was the only way he knew how to apologize. It was like he wanted me to forget what he had done.

Instead of moving out right away, it took me several weeks to regain enough strength to make the transition. Paul intuitively knew I was planning on leaving so he suggested we exchange vehicles daily so I could take the dogs to the beach in his Escalade. Paul was trying to prevent the inevitable. About a week later, I had an appointment with my therapist, Sandy, and she encouraged me to leave him.

I luckily had my car the day I met with her. I came home from our appointment, took a scolding hot shower, and waited a few minutes on the settee in the study to summon enough courage to pack my things. I remember packing my car, throwing my clothes and shoes in it, running to and fro, terrified Paul might come home. My Lexus was in a state of disarray, clothes were in no order what so ever. Each time I took armfuls of stuff to the car, I prayed to God, "Please don't let Paul come home early." If he came home in the middle of my moving, I had no idea what he would do.

I kissed my dogs goodbye and started the drive to L.A. Paul realized I left approximately an hour after I did. He went home, noticed all my things gone, and tracked my phone using the Find My Phone app on our joint cellular account. He got in his Escalade and tried to catch up with me on the 101 Freeway. He never did, but he repeatedly called and texted me for the next couple days.

Paul said, "You're making a huge mistake, Michelle." He urged me to come back and be with him. He fed me a bunch of bullshit that I soaked up. "You will come running back to me because you will eventually realize that you will never find a man as great as me again, Michelle."

He was right, not about the part of him being a great man, but about me running back to him. My therapist told me to leave, but I didn't have the courage to stay away for any extended period of time. It was almost like a sick addiction that made me keep going back to Paul. I knew deep down in my soul that Paul was a sadistic, abusive man, but I got to the point where I thought I needed him.

I continued allowing him to control my life. It was like craving your drug of choice before having serious withdrawals. The first time you take a hit, you don't need much, but then you grow a tolerance, and you can take more and more. I tolerated the comments, the physical abuse and the emotional manipulation.

I felt sick, tired and overwhelmed by our destructive relationship. Family and friends asked me questions about why I kept leaving and going back. No one knew the torment I endured. I kept my mouth shut and didn't tell anyone. I made up stories similar to the truth but never entirely accurate.

"We just had an argument, we need a break, and we're working it out."

"It was my fault, I knew he was stressed, I shouldn't have said anything to trigger him."

Excuse after excuse after excuse came out of my mouth. I lied to my family, my friends, and to myself.

Chapter Ten: The Honeymoon Phase

August 2013 - May 2014

According to Psychologist and author Lenore Walker, Ed.D, "Battering is not a 'fight' that involves two people. Often, violence will be triggered by something utterly insignificant."

Paul's outbursts were often prompted by a comment, a look, or sometimes absolutely nothing. I had no idea how to predict the monster. When I finally thought all was good, I would run into a solid brick wall. I needed help.

In August of 2013, I started to see Dr. Matt as well. He was located in Los Angeles so it was easy for me to regularly see him. I went to therapy once a week pretty consistently. Paul and I did couples counseling a few times, and this enabled me to thoroughly explain the abuse. I showed Paul the photos of my face from the October incident in a therapy session one time. Dr. Matt felt that Paul would learn from this experience. Paul said, "I want to beat up whoever did that to you, I can't remember doing any of it." To Paul, it seemed as if I were explaining the beatings I received from another person, not him.

According to *The Domestic Violence Sourcebook,* a psychiatric clinical nurse whose job was to identify and assist battered women believes that "professional women who remain in abusive relationships tend to believe that their partners will change through therapy-and that these women often make the mistake of entering couples therapy." The problems abusers experience in their lives need to be addressed separately from the victims. An abuser has abuse and/or psychological damage that needs to be remedied prior to couples therapy. Dr. Matt voiced many times that Paul was in denial, that he was not taking full responsibility for his actions. Dr. Matt consistently questioned me as to why I wanted to stay with a man who beat me, manipulated me, and emotionally abused me. My answer was always the same…

"But I love him."

Dr. Matt suggested that Paul and I take a seminar with Landmark, an organization that promised to "redefine what's possible in your relationships, your work, your family, your communities, what matters most to you." Dr. Matt told us, "If you go through Landmark, it could save you two years of therapy." Paul was all about saving time and money, so we went. The Landmark Forum is a weekend seminar where the instructors question your thinking. It makes you look at different ways of living. "The Landmark Forum offers a practical methodology for producing breakthroughs—achievements that are extraordinary, outside of what's predictable," according to their website.

The weekend was incredibly uplifting. What I learned was I was in love with the *idea* of love. I withstood far too much when I should have ran in the opposite direction. I desperately wanted a fairy tale romance, but what I had was a tumultuous, dangerous, destructive, and co-dependent conjunction. I needed to release my imaginary truth and accept reality—I was in a romantic relationship with a narcissistic man who would never fully appreciate me.

I learned I stayed with Paul because I subconsciously thought I didn't deserve better. I thought the attention I received from Paul was as good as it got. I used the expression, "The grass isn't always greener on the other side." But it was. The grass was luscious and blooming with a wide spectrum of purple wild flowers.

Paul and I decided to continue our education with Landmark and took the entire curriculum, which was approximately six months long. During our teachings, Paul and I got along better than we ever had. He said, "I'm learning a lot about us, Michelle. I'm sorry I was such an ass to you." He promised things would change, and they did...for a while.

He and I had great moments together and I dreamt he would overcome his issues and we could have the relationship I desired. We remained in a long-distance relationship and saw each other almost weekly. I got a job in L.A. as a bartender so I didn't have to rely on Paul for my every need. I also got an agent and started acting again.

Paul told me, "I'd like to start a business with you, Michelle." He wanted to invest in a cold-pressed juice company and have me run it. I loved the idea. He and I talked a lot about the details. He wanted to give me part ownership and I was excited. Paul said, "I know you love acting, but if that doesn't work out, you can have this as a backup plan."

I began to see the characteristics I fell in love with. He was encouraging, charming, and supportive. We'd stay on the phone for hours talking about our day. He'd say, "When we are married in a few years, we will be able to travel the world." I relished in the thought.

We had very memorable nights together. Sometimes, we would walk through Walmart, buy Sour Patch Kids and M&Ms to sneak into the movie theater, and watch a movie while holding each other and throwing popcorn at one another like children. After the movie, we'd wait in the drive through at In-N-Out Burger, order double doubles, milkshakes, and fries, and laugh at what piglets we were being.

Sometimes Paul was very romantic. He'd call me out of the blue and say, "I'm coming to see you." He'd pick me up at home and surprise me with a fancy dinner and a basketball game. We'd stay at a hotel downtown L.A. and watch a romantic movie like *The Notebook* or *Titanic*.

On April 11, 2014, we went to a seminar called "Spring Leadership" in Las Vegas. It was a reunion of sorts with a lot of our old leadership friends. We heard many of the leaders speak about what they accomplished in the past year. We stayed for a few hours then Paul said, "Let's go gamble." We stayed up late sitting at blackjack tables playing hundred dollar hands. I lost more than I won, but Paul didn't get upset with me.

In May, Paul hired a private airline for our needs. He paid a flat fee every month for us to be able to use the plane whenever we wanted to go anywhere in California or Las Vegas. It was awesome flying in a private jet. Paul said, "We deserve this," and told me to pack my bags.

Our first destination was Santa Barbara. We stayed at the Ritz-Carlton Bacara Resort right next to the Pacific Ocean. The property had three pools, five restaurants, and a spa. He and I stayed late in the jacuzzi and drank wine in our room by the fireplace all night. We woke up to birds chirping and the sound of the ocean outside our window. We went to breakfast and he told me, "I love you so much," Michelle." I was overcome with happiness.

Paul stayed consistent with Landmark and attended almost all the weekly meetings in Culver City. I felt things really changed. Paul asked me, "Do you want to move back home?" I immediately said, "Yes!" Paul's dazzling, infectious self didn't last but for brief periods of time between his toxic, corrupt, and poisoning tantrums. This nine-month stretch was the longest we went without any physical violence. When things were good, I would cherish every moment, but when things got bad, they got ugly.

Chapter Eleven: Therapy Didn't Help

June 2014

In June, Paul and I went to dinner at our favorite restaurant in town. As soon as we were seated, I ordered a shot of Don Julio 1942 and Paul ordered his typical Vodka Red Bull. We shared a bottle of Tolosa Pinot Noir and ate grass-fed, melt-in-your-mouth filet mignons. After dinner, I asked the server, "Can we have two cappuccinos and the Butterfinger pie, please?" This was our favorite desert. It was a Butterfinger ice cream cake with an Oreo cookie crust that was drizzled with warm caramel. Paul was in an exceptional mood and our evening consisted of great food, amazing sex, and falling asleep in each other's arms.

I couldn't stay asleep though. I woke up at 3 a.m. tossing and turning trying to go back to dreamland, but couldn't. I didn't want to disturb Paul, so I quietly took a pillow and went out to the living room to lay on the couch and watch a movie. His computer was sitting on the end table and I opened it to browse the Internet. As soon as I logged on, Paul's Facebook profile popped up. I'm not sure what possessed me, but I started snooping through his social media account.

I opened his messages and started reading. I read a conversation between a woman and Paul. They were chatting about some young, brunette girl from the local college. My heart sank. My pulse started racing, my blood started boiling, and I forced myself to read on. I read Paul and this girl were having an affair, but Paul ended it recently. My blood pressure sky rocketed. I was so incredibly pissed and let down. I had stayed by his side faithfully for two and a half years while he worked on his issues. I stayed through the abuse, the manipulation, and the lies, but cheating was something I couldn't take.

I had to stop reading. With sweat on my hands, I went to the bedroom, turned on the light, threw the covers off of him, and said, "Get your ass out of bed!" At this point, I was so upset that I didn't care what Paul would do to me if I started a fight. He, of course, pretended not to know what I was talking about. He was screaming at me for waking him up to "this foolish nonsense."

"What the hell are you doing? You are delirious, Michelle!"

He eventually confessed about the infidelity and blamed it on me. He said, "You should have known I would do this, you weren't in town enough to satisfy my needs." He also suggested I was doing the same in L.A. He said, "It doesn't matter anyway, now we are even." The biggest issue with his statement was that it was 100 percent false. I was faithful to him for our entire relationship.

He conceded that there were two other one-night stands as well. He told me he ended the affairs in April because he realized how much he loved me. Paul said, "I was planning on telling you tonight until you started drinking tequila." I didn't believe him.

I was a complete mess. For the next several nights, I drank an entire fifth of Maker's Mark, rolled around on the kitchen floor, and cried hysterically. Paul tried to console me. He brought pillows into the kitchen and laid down on the floor with me. He profusely apologized.

"I really didn't think you would react like this, I'm sorry."

Of all the things he did to me, this is what hurt me the most. All his friends knew this woman and did not tell me about the affair; they smiled and acted normal every time I was in town. I was humiliated, devastated, and emotionally wounded. He told me, "I never thought my affair would have such an impact on you." I guess he thought if I put up with all the violence, I could also put up with the infidelity. He truly believed we would work through it and everything would be fine.

Paul tried desperately to keep me around. He swore, "The affairs didn't mean anything and I will never cheat on you again." I was in a state of shock and couldn't decide what to do.

I stayed at his house for the next two weeks. On June 20, we went to dinner with his family at a steakhouse in town. Paul started drinking heavily and I wasn't watching his consumption. I was fully immersed in my misery and didn't pay attention to what Paul was doing. June 2014 meant that it had been nearly a year since he last physically assaulted me, so I didn't think anything of it. I was too hurt to care about much of anything.

We got back to the house and Paul continued drinking. His younger brother left with his mom. It was just Paul, Jack and me that remained. Jack asked me, "Are you going to be okay with Paul alone?" Jack knew about the affairs and some of the violence that happened. I assured him, "I trust Paul won't hurt me; we've been through too much therapy," so Jack left.

Paul and I started talking and I brought up the affairs. I began to cry and said, "You are such an ass for cheating on me, Paul!" Something snapped in his mind and I saw the blue in his eyes disappear yet again. I was sitting on the love seat next to the overarching lamp I replaced after the October fight. He grabbed the lamp and tore it out of the wall, throwing it over my head. I stood and started backing up towards the door. He recognized what I was doing, came towards me, gripped the collar of my shirt, and tore it and my bra right off of my body.

He put his hands around my throat and threw me on the bed in our room, just off to the right of the entryway. He squeezed my esophagus hard while I struggled for oxygen. This incident lasted roughly ten minutes before he realized what he was doing. This was a big improvement from the three to five-hour long beatings I endured in the past, but still long enough to kill me. He looked at me in utter shock and said, "You triggered me, Michelle," and walked away.

I slept on the couch, fearful to leave or do anything that would set him off again. We didn't speak until the next morning. He said, "I feel humiliated I let myself get to that point again."

I told him, "I need a break and I'm gonna go see my family." Paul understood and let me go.

While I was visiting my family, I told them that Paul had an affair. However, I didn't tell them about the emotional and physical abuse. My mom said, "That's totally unacceptable." I thought to myself, "If they only knew what was going on behind closed doors, my dad would hang Paul by the balls." I was too ashamed to disclose those pertinent details.

In August, I flew to Kenya on a mission trip I had scheduled months prior. I went with an organization based in Portland to help children at a primary school near Nairobi. Paul encouraged me to still go even though I was distraught. He said, "It might help you heal." Essentially he thought if I witnessed the extreme poverty in a third world country, I would become awaken to the fact that Paul was a great man. It didn't work.

I had a lot of time to think about Paul while I was there. I started to slowly forgive him, but realized our relationship was unhealthy and potentially life threatening. While I was away, Paul wrote me an email:

Aug 15, 2014

"i hope you know how much i respect and admire everything are doing right now. i am so proud that you are tanking the reigns in life and walking the path you are choosing, you have chosen to walk from some things that weren't serving you in the way you could be YOU and now look, your stronger and sexier than ever, too me at least.

i want to let you know i love you widely and deeply and support you exclusively because of that love and belief in who you are and what you are trying to and will accomplish.

we've been through allot, we've both been on the hurting side and have also been the one giving the hurt, me more so than you. and i want you to know i am sorry, and i truly understand your emotional response to what has happened with us, and what I've caused between us. i also want you to know i love you regardless of how you have been treating me, and I get it.

i don't think many, could imagine being with a better more loyal, loving, caring, sexy, beautiful, talented, funny, godly, passionate, empathetic, womanly, and " horny" woman than you, and thats why i love you and have stayed in this relationship, regardless of my mistakes for as long as i have ..

i want to build something with you michelle thats special and that lasts for eternity ... something we can do on earth together that will forever live, and that our souls will inherit in the future, in heaven. i know you have some things to think on, and we both have some things to talk about and i want you to know I'm committed to you just as you are committed to me what ever way and context that is.

love you with all my heart for ever .. can't wait to talk and hear from you"

At first glance, the email seemed loving, but when I looked deep, I could see he still blamed me for the abuse and infidelities. He didn't take any responsibility for what he had done. Going to Kenya helped me realize that the constant communication between Paul and I was not healthy. I started to grasp how diseased our relationship was.

Kenya was an amazing experience coupled with heartbreak and sadness. The people were affectionate and expressed how much they wanted me to stay there. They told me stories of their struggles, which were riddled with hunger and abuse. Some of the issues in the village could be fixed rather quickly, but the organization didn't have the funds. A young girl sat on my lap the day we left the primary school. She begged me, "Take me with you." All I could do was cry.

I came back from my trip the end of August. Paul and I tried to work it out, but eventually decided to just stay friends. We continued to talk every day, so nothing really seemed to change. It was as if we were still in a romantic relationship, just without the sex.

Chapter Twelve: Still Friends

Fall/Winter 2014

Paul said, "I still want to help you, Michelle." In the beginning of our relationship, Paul asked me to add his name to all of my credit cards and use those credit cards for everything including his bills, our dinners, and car insurance premiums. He wanted me to keep using the credit cards for all my expenses, even though we were technically not in a romantic relationship any longer. He said, "I want to keep the joint credit cards as my way of supporting you and taking care of you."

Paul was financially abusing me by controlling my resources. I asked him, "Will you please pay off the debt like you promised so I can move on?" It never happened. He said, "Paying off the debt is not my priority right now, Michelle. It'll happen when I'm ready." He made me worry about the debt incessantly.

In return for him "taking care of me," I was to do personal assistant duties such as scheduling appointments, writing emails, and giving him reminders. The arrangement was I would work from home for him. I'd use the credit cards for all expenses and he would pay them each month. Essentially this was Paul's tactic to keep me under his control. Paul stole my independence, causing me to continue being dependent on him, and I let it happen.

He'd mishandle our finances, which caused me to stress out about our credit card debt every month. I learned that credit card companies do not report late payments to the credit bureaus until the payment is sixty days late. I called him every month saying, "Paul, baby, it's time to put money in the account so I can make minimum payments." He'd get angry and sometimes push the envelope, waiting until day fifty-eight before making minimum payments, just to piss me off.

I believe that men inherently want to take care of their significant others. Healthy men love to spoil women as long as the women are appreciative of their gift. Unhealthy men, however, tend to use money as a way to control and harass women. Paul and I were $45,000 in credit card debt, not including the Lexus, insurance premiums, mortgage, and rent. I felt trapped. I couldn't make Paul pay off the debt, and if I walked away, I was scared to lose my good credit score. I was really fearful of how I was going to manage without Paul and looking back, I think that was his strategy. So I reluctantly stayed in constant communication with him.

In September, Paul told me, "I want you to come with me to Minnesota for my business partner's wedding as part of our deal. I'll pay for the trip. Just take care of the necessities." I requested the days off from my part-time bar job and went with him for the weekend.

The wedding was high profile and it was essential that I wore an evening gown. Paul took me shopping at The Mall of America where he bought me a beautiful black Cache dress. He said, "Make an appointment to get your hair and nails done, put it on the credit card." I looked like a million bucks. I felt like a princess that night as we laughed with one another and danced to 90s music. The trip went well, without a hitch.

Memories flooded my mind. It was times like the trip to Minnesota where I really missed Paul. I missed the fun-loving, carefree Paul. The one that wouldn't hurt a fly. The one who laid with me on our couch watching animated cartoons while we laughed and ate Taco Bell.

The problem was Paul also possessed a side to him that was toxic and poisonous. I knew through trial and error that Paul could kill me. I thought about the abuse and asked God, "Why is he like this? Why can't he be better?"

I never heard God's answer.

According to *The Domestic Violence Sourcebook,* "The control skills used by a batterer have been found by researchers to strongly resemble the brainwashing techniques practiced by Nazi concentration camp soldiers and prisoner of war guards. Of course, most batterers have no formal awareness of the techniques they are using, yet they know how to use isolation, torture, and violence to destroy the will and spirit of another human being." Paul had alternating personalities that would switch at a moment's notice. He would be the most loving, caring, amazing man, then transform suddenly as if he were possessed by a demon.

Paul asked me at the end of September, "Do you want to drive up for a few nights and spend time with the dogs and me at the beach?" I replied, "Yeah, I miss Dodger and Steele." During the afternoon on Saturday, we went to the dog beach and threw balls into the ocean and watched our Siberian Husky dive to recover them. Our chihuahua hated the water, so he pranced around like he was a king, avoiding the tides. It was fun spending the afternoon in the sun.

We were only friends but the romantic feelings were still there. I think we both wanted a relationship to ensue, but each time we got close, Paul would do something to extinguish the flame. I knew I was in danger by staying with Paul. I knew if I didn't get out for good, he would seriously hurt me or even kill me. I couldn't figure out how to break free from the toxic cycle I was in.

That night, we went to a local bar with a group of people. I don't remember what set Paul off, but at some point in the night, he grabbed my arm and started leading me out in the streets towards his car. I got scared and tried to run while wearing five-inch stilettos, I didn't make it far before Paul caught up to me. A stranger on the street asked, "Are you alright, miss?" Before I could say anything, Paul answered, "She's fine."

One of Paul's friends had come with us to the bar. Terry was also a potential business partner of Paul's. He was African American, approximately 5'8" with a witty smile. Terry left the bar when he noticed we had exited. Thank God he caught up with us on the street. I begged Terry, "Will you please come back to the house with us?" He did. At the house, Terry stood in the doorway of the guest bedroom holding Paul back from attacking me. Paul was so angry with me for absolutely nothing. Paul yelled at Terry, "Get the hell out of my way." He pushed Terry to the side, grabbed the end of the bed and snapped the footboard off the rails. I was sitting on the bed terrified. Terry jumped up and held Paul back before Paul could get to me.

I tried apologizing to him through my sobs. It didn't work in the past so I don't know why I thought it would work now. "It's my fault, Paul, I'm sorry," I said. Paul screamed, "I don't fucking care, Michelle. Get your shit and get the fuck out!"

I got up to leave, but he wouldn't let me. He stood in the doorway blocking the exit while Terry watched. Paul threatened me, "I'm gonna call the police if you leave and I'm gonna tell them you are driving drunk." I ignored him, but when I tried to move toward the door, he said, "If you leave, you have to give me your clothes, shoes, and phone since I paid for them. They are my property, not yours." I attempted to undress but that infuriated him more.

I stayed in the guest bedroom with Terry and Paul for over two hours while Paul berated me, scolding me for upsetting him. If Terry hadn't been there, I know Paul would have beaten me for hours. Once Paul calmed down, I slept on the couch in fear. I thought if I left, Paul would catch me and beat me. The next morning, Paul and Terry left the house to get Jamba Juice for breakfast. I rushed to my car, and drove ninety down the 101 Freeway back to L.A.

A month later, Paul asked me, "Do you want to go to a game with me? I'll be on my best behavior." I missed him. Although he always managed to screw things up, I still wanted to see him. I said, "That'd be awesome, Paul. Thank you."

Super Bowl Sunday has been considered the day of dread for female victims of domestic violence, according to some experts. Nearly four million women were physically abused by their husbands or boyfriends in 2000 on Super Bowl Sunday.

Although Paul and I never went to the Super Bowl, we did attend one of the largest sporting events in baseball...the Playoffs.

I met Paul at his hotel and we scheduled a driver to take us to Game 2 of the 2014 National League Division Series between the Los Angeles Dodgers and the St. Louis Cardinals at Dodger Stadium. I was nervous about joining him, but Paul assured me that nothing would happen. I believed him, like an idiot. We were dressed in Dodgers gear from head to toe, both in baseball caps and jerseys. He and I sat in amazing seats with access to the VIP lounge where they served an endless supply of liquor, beer, and wine.

Towards the end of the game, I noticed Paul and I had consumed three or four drinks a piece. The Dodger's won the game and Paul wanted to celebrate. He said, "We should go back to the lounge and have victory drinks!" I didn't want to go, but reluctantly followed him. We scheduled his driver to pick us up at 9:30 p.m., and when the driver arrived, I closed out the bar tab, which infuriated Paul. I told him, "I'm ready to go." He started yelling at me in front of all the people in the lounge.

"You are stupid, Michelle. The driver can wait, that's what I pay him for. You had no right to close the tab, idiot."

I was mortified and scared. Paul led me out of the lounge by my arm before I could communicate to the bar staff that I was in danger. I broke free from Paul's grip and ran, hiding behind cars in the stadium parking lot. After all the cars left, I hesitantly took a cab to Paul's hotel. I didn't want to face him, but my purse and bag were in his room, and my car was parked with the valet. I had to go get my things.

When I arrived, I asked the valet for my car and they informed me that Paul took the keys. I then walked up to the room and put the hotel key card in the slot. The red lights flashed. I inserted the room key again with no luck. Paul changed the key cards and locked me out of the room. I went to the reception desk to ask if I could get a new room key and they said, "I'm sorry Ms.

Jewsbury, but your name is not registered on the room."

I walked across the street to see if Paul was at the nearby bar. I thought if I begged him for my things, he would give them back. I decided he couldn't hurt me in a public place.

I stumbled into him crossing the other direction on my way to the bar. He started hollering at me. "How the hell did you get here, Michelle?" I told him I took a cab so I could get my things. He screamed, "What things? I own you, Michelle."

We were downtown Los Angeles, on the corner of a very busy street, yelling for over an hour. I was getting nowhere with him. I finally flagged a cab to take me to my apartment in the San Fernando Valley before Paul could make any attempt at stopping me.

The next morning, I knew I had to do something. I called Paul and said, "Look, I know I upset you when I closed your bar tab last night, but I should at least be able to get my purse back." He disagreed so I said, "You're right, I am an idiot." This was just a ploy to get my stuff back. He told me, "Come back to my hotel room so we can talk."

I arrived at the hotel and took the elevator to the eleventh floor. My heart was pounding and sweat began beading on my hands. I knocked, knowing I might be in trouble. Paul opened the door and said, "Come in," We didn't talk. Instead, we laid on the bed watching a baseball game together.

"I need my stuff, and I wonder where he put the key to my car?" I thought. I didn't want to upset him so I stayed silent. My inner monologue told me that I was in danger and needed to find a way out. My thoughts were a conglomerate distorted mess. I thought about how much I cared about him and asked myself, "Why? How could I still love a man that treats me like this?"

When the game was over, Paul said, "Let's go to Yard House to get some lunch." I was able to retrieve my belongings and my car after we ate. I drove him to the private jet center in Hawthorne where he had reserved a flight to Santa Barbara. He took his plane and I took my car and my belongings. We never discussed what happened.

From then on, I tried to limit any time with him. Unfortunately, I had a hard time cutting him out of my life completely. He had brainwashed me to believe I needed him. I talked with him on the phone and answered his texts, but did not make any attempts at seeing him. Paul said, "I want to continue helping you financially until you get on your feet." I was well aware that his "help" was a form of deranged control, but I was looking for a way out.

On November 1, 2014, Paul sent me flowers with two cards. They read:

"This is a start...I love you and I am sorry...and I am grate[ful] to have you in my life. I hope this brightens your day! Love - Me :)"

"Each of these roses is the [number of] apologies I owe and the gratitude I plan to extend to you for you being lovely, caring, loyal, and behind me through thick and thin since our start! You're beautiful beyond measure."

I thought the gesture was sweet, but I knew the flowers didn't represent his acknowledgment of being a dick. On November 4, I made an appointment with a lawyer. I learned about domestic violence and about the law. I primarily sought legal assistance regarding palimony for my credit card debt, but was advised to press charges for assault and battery. However, I declined.

For two months I didn't see Paul. I would call and remind him to go to the bank or pay the dogwalker, but I didn't go back. Slowly but surely I was beginning to feel independent again.

During Christmas, I flew home to Idaho to spend time with my family. My dad and I hit the slopes, but there wasn't enough snow on the mountain. I told Dad, "It's gonna be fine, don't worry." I thought going down an un-groomed, double black diamond off the face of Schweitzer Mountain was a good idea. I toppled. I fell, and I fell hard. I was taken down the mountain in a toboggan by an attractive ski instructor that teased me the whole way down. "You sure did a dandy, miss," he said. I learned I had torn my ACL and that my injury would require surgery.

After Paul found out what happened, he told our friend Janelle he wanted to "support me" for another six months. Janelle worked for Landmark until Paul hired her as an in-house counselor. She was a very smart woman from Egypt. Janelle was half black, half Israeli, super tall with freckles all over her face. She was very beautiful. I spoke to Janelle all the time. I told her about the violence between Paul and I, and she told me, "You need to get out, Michelle." She and I were devising a plan.

Paul insisted on paying for my ACL reconstructive surgery. I told him, "I don't want to take your money," but there was no arguing with Paul. I felt that I couldn't turn him down. I thought that if I said no, he would somehow come after me, cut me out of his life, or something worse. I know this doesn't make sense, but I allowed him to continue financially manipulating me. I subconsciously knew he would use his financial control against me, but I was holding on to the last shred of hope at mending our mangled relationship. I was frustrated, hopeless, and frazzled.

Surgery was scheduled for Thursday, January 29. My mom flew to L.A. Monday, January 26 to help me recover after surgery. The lease of my 2012 Lexus was about to expire, so Paul offered to lease me another vehicle before I underwent the operation. My mom and I met Paul at the Lexus dealership in Santa Barbara on Tuesday to exchange the car for a 2015 lease. This was the first time in months I saw Paul face to face. He was very cordial and charming. He even told my mom, "You look beautiful, Wendy." We signed the papers and my mom and I left with a brand new car.

I was recovering well after surgery so my mom and I wanted to go see my uncle in Las Vegas on February 6 for a few days. Paul insisted, "Use the plane." I happily took the offer. On the drive to the airstrip, he called me to see how we were doing. He was on speakerphone in the car and about sixty seconds into the conversation I asked him if he would go to the bank to make a deposit so our credit cards wouldn't be late. He started screaming at me while on speakerphone with my mom in the car. "What more do you fucking want, Michelle?" I hung up on him.

I didn't tell my mom about the beatings or the verbal attacks and I didn't want her to hear his mistreatment of me. I never told her because I was ashamed. My mom raised me to never accept this type of treatment from anyone. I didn't want my mom to know I had been tolerating Paul's abuse for over three years.

Paul called Surfair and canceled our flight. I called him back to try and persuade him to reconsider, allowing him to scream at me for fifteen minutes on speakerphone while my mom heard everything. "I'll take care of the damn credit cards, Michelle. I just leased you a brand new fucking Lexus. You should be kissing my ass right now." And so on. I was unsuccessful in trying to get him to change his mind. We never ended up seeing my uncle.

My mom started balling hysterically as soon as I hung up the phone. She didn't realize Paul had such an evil side to him and immediately became frightened for my life and well-being. I felt compelled to tell her everything—all his erraticism, misconduct, and wrongdoings. I finally told her, "Paul beat me a few times, Mom. He talks to me like this all the time." I didn't disclose all details, but I let her know I was in trouble. I was trapped in a cycle of fear and abuse. I told her, "He is controlling me and I don't know how to escape."

She begged me, "Stay away from him and get out of the mess you are in, Michelle." Unfortunately, the mess was a lot harder to get out of than she thought.

Janelle called me after my mom flew home and said, "Paul wants to meet and talk about the car." Paul needed to send in one last piece of paper and he was holding it over my head. Janelle said, "I will be with you the whole time and you can stay with me after we talk to him," so I took a train and headed up north. Paul agreed he would send in the paperwork and pay for the lease. We agreed to end our relationship for good. That night, while sleeping at Janelle's, I showed her the photos of my face from the October beating. She said, "If you press charges, you are sure to win." I said, "I don't know if I can do that."

On March 27, Paul was on a business trip so I drove up to see my dogs for the night. I took them on a hike and to the dog beach. We played catch until the sun went down. I let them sleep with me in the bed, something Paul forbid. The dogs intuitively knew that something was wrong the next day. Paul wouldn't let me take Dodger and Steele to L.A., and even if I wanted to, I had nowhere to keep a Siberian Husky. I told Steele, "Bye, boy, be a good dog for Paul," while warm tears were streaming down my face. He licked me and I walked out the front door.

There are so many reasons why women return to abusive relationships. It is widely known that victims may leave their abuser seven times before permanently escaping, according to *The National Domestic Violence Hotline*. A Texas study indicates that 75 percent of women who called a domestic violence hotline left their abuser at least five times. I left Paul so many times I lost count. It would take me another eight months of planning and reaching out for help before I could stay away for good.

According to the Domestic Abuse Intervention Project of Duluth, Minnesota, certain behaviors of abusive men have been identified. Some characteristics of the early stages of abuse that precede physical battering are listed here. Women who recognize several of these traits in their partners should take a good look at the relationship, and carefully consider getting out before it becomes violent.

1. *Your partner has a history go growing up in a violent family, a setting where he learned that violence is normal behavior.*

2. He has a tendency to use force or violence to try and solve problems- as indicated by behavior such as a criminal record for violence, a quick temper or tendency to overreact to minor frustrations, fighting, destructive behavior when angry, cruelty to animals.
3. He abuses alcohol or drugs.
4. He has a poor image of himself, often masked by trying to act tough.
5. He often exhibits jealousy, not only of other men, but also of friends and family members.
6. He exhibits hypermasculine behavior- he feels he should make all the decisions, tell you what your role as a woman and his as a man must be. He has very traditional ideas about appropriate roles and behaviors of men and women, and thinks women are second-class citizens. He expects you to follow his orders and advice and may become angry if you can't read his mind and anticipate what he wants.
7. He emotionally abuses you or other women with name-calling, putdowns, humiliation, and attempts to create guilt.
8. He isolates you by telling you who you may see or talk to, controls what you do and where you go, even what you read. He keeps tabs on your every move and wants you with him all the time.
9. He intimidates you and makes you afraid through looks, anger, actions, a display of weapons or gestures. He destroys your property or abuses your pets. He enjoys playing with lethal weapons and threatens to use them against those he feels wronged him. You do what he wants you to do and constantly work to keep him from getting angry.
10. He portrays "Jekyll and Hyde" behavior. He goes through highs and lows, as though he is two different people, and he swings from extremely kind to extremely cruel.
11. He uses coercion and threats. He tells you he will hurt you, leave you, or kill himself if you leave. If you file charges against him, he makes you drop them by threatening violence or suicide. Have you changed your life so you won't make him angry?
12. He treats you roughly, and physically forces you to do things you do not want to do.

13. *He often denies his actions, minimizing or making light of his own abusive behavior, refusing to take your concerns seriously, and blaming you for his behavior.*
14. *He economically abuses you by preventing you from getting or keeping a job, controlling all the money in the household, making you ask for money, or concealing his income.*
15. *Weapons are important to him as instruments of power or control, he is unusually fascinated with guns or other weapons, without or beyond any reasonable explanation for such an interest (such as collecting antiques, historical reenactment, or hunting).*
16. *He has battered or stalked a partner in a prior relationship and/or has a history of police encounters fro assault, battery, threats, or stalking.*
17. *He tried to inappropriately accelerate his relationship with you when you were dating, prematurely discussing marriage or other commitment, then expects the relationship to last forever, no matter what may happen.*
18. *He refers to his use of alcohol or drugs as an excuse for hostile or violent behavior.*
19. *He can't accept rejection, resists change or compromise, is generally inflexible.*
20. *He is not just devoted, but obsessed with you; he spends a disproportionate amount of time talking about you, watching, or following you, and derives much of his identity from being your partner.*
21. *He is paranoid, believes others are out to get him, and projects strong emotional feelings such as hate or jealousy onto others when there is no evidence that would lead a reasonable person to perceive such emotions. .*
22. *He refuses to take responsibility for his own actions, and always blames others for problems of his own making.*
23. *He is usually moody, sullen, depressed, or any about something.*
24. *He tries to enlist your friends and family in his own campaign to keep you with him or get you back if you have left.*
25. *Perhaps most important of all: If you have an intuitive feeling that you are at risk from this man, if you fear he might injure or kill you, listen to your own instincts!*

Chapter Thirteen: Grief

May - December 2015

On May 26, 2015, my father passed away unexpectedly. He had a blood clotting disorder related to his Intervene Thrombosis and at approximately 6 p.m., he was watching television in the living room and a blood clot in one of the deep veins in his leg broke free, causing him to have a sudden and instantaneous heart attack. His death was extremely difficult for my family. Paul called me, "I'm so sorry for your loss, Michelle. If there's anything I can do, let me know."

My mom hated Paul and refused to allow him to come to the funeral. Paul sent a large bouquet of flowers to the funeral home, but never attempted a flight to Idaho. Although my mom said, "Don't have any contact with the asshole," I spoke to Paul regularly on the phone. I was in shock and the familiarity of Paul's voice helped soothe me.

I started therapy again with Dr. Matt shortly after my father passed away. He helped me deal with the grief of losing my dad and exposed me yet again to the wounds I possessed because of Paul. When Paul raised his voice, it made me feel inadequate and fearful. Every time a man raised his voice in anger, my heart would start fluttering and I'd have a minor anxiety attack. I was unable to drive with a man in the passenger seat of my car for quite some time because of Paul's verbal abuse. Dr. Matt diagnosed me with Post Traumatic Stress Disorder and Battered Woman's Syndrome and advised me to start taking care of myself and quit talking to Paul.

I had hit rock bottom. I reached my breaking point. My dad's death and the anguish from being tormented for over three years from Paul brought me to a new consciousness. I couldn't take it anymore. The physical, emotional, and financial abuse were too much. It was time for a rebirth, a metamorphosis into a new beginning. I was deeply burdened by pain, resentment, animosity, and cynicism. I needed a way to remedy and fix my soul.

I started writing about my experience. Dr. Matt said, "Writing is a good way to truly see everything that happened to you." I wrote from a wound, not yet a scar, so the first draft of this book had nothing to do with love and everything to do with hate. I hated Paul. I hated him for deflating my imaginary, storybook fairy tale romance, for hurting me to the deepest part of my core. I resented the day I ever met Paul and I was extremely bitter. I did a few re-writes that included the love I had for him. I eventually forgave him for the abuse.

I began writing a solo play based on the violence I experienced while with Paul. I worked with Jessica Lynn Johnson, a director and actor awarded Best National Solo Artist by the Dialogue One Festival. Rehearsals were the toughest. I played both Paul and myself. I repeated his words every day and I essentially beat myself up on stage. It was extremely difficult, but the play helped me overcome what I had gone through. It helped me heal.

I felt sympathy for Paul. Through therapy and writing, I started to feel compassion instead of hate. I attributed his anger issues to not dealing with his past; therefore, he took his aggression out on me. I learned the abuse was not my fault.

The Domestic Violence Sourcebook has help for batterers. A Maryland psychologist named Steven Stosny developed a program based on the theory that most batterers can't sustain attachments. They become overwhelmed with feelings of shame, guilt, and abandonment, which they seek to manage through aggression. He created a five-step program, called "HEALS." This technique effectively teaches, "Mr. Hyde to remember what Dr. Jekyll learned." This twelve-week program has an 86 percent effective rate of the participants having ending physical abuse a year after treatment, and 73 percent success rate of having ended emotional and verbal abuse.

The technique starts with the concept that compassion is true power, blame is powerless, and there is room to "Heal." The next step in Stosny's program is that men are taught to "Explain" to themselves their personal hurt and pain masked by their anger that leads to abusive behavior. Then they are taught to "Apply" mercy and give themselves grace instead of assaulting their partner with physical or verbal abuse. The men are directed to move into a feeling of "Love" for his partner and himself; therefore, being able to speak their mind without attacking their companion; love and compassion instead of anger and abuse. Lastly, this technique will "Solve the Problem" of abuse.

There are three points that many experts agree are essential for the successful healing of abusers. Admitting responsibility for the abuse is a requirement. It is necessary for him to realize what he did was wrong, understand he can't control people, and truly want to make a change. Second, there needs to be a consequence for his actions. Those consequences can vary from jail time to fines to court ordered treatment programs. The third point that experts agree upon is accountability. Through group therapy, probation, counseling or a court order strictly prohibiting violence with definitive disciplinary actions, the abuser can stay accountable.

I personally think that for Paul, a public display of compassion, voicing his responsibility for his actions, and voluntarily offering assistance to other abusers would be beneficial. However, Paul has not taken responsibility for what he did. Any time I brought up abuse, he would reshape specific details and name me the culprit and the problem. I began to heal and his versions of the "episodes" seemed very inaccurate. Paul was in denial. He and I continued to speak on the phone because I needed him to pay off our jointly held debt. He refused to pay off the bills in order to keep me in his life, even though he had moved on to another woman.

There is a consensus among domestic violence and mental health professionals that partner abuse is a learned behavior. They learn that, through intimidation and manipulation, they have the power to control their partner. This behavior can be learned through social, economic, or household situations. Battering is not a psychopathology and the majority of batterers will exhibit minor, if any, psychiatric limitations, according to specialists. Most men who batter women typically abuse more than one. In one study, 95 percent of men who sought treatment admitted to abusing more than one woman.

Paul started dating a young, beautiful, blonde woman in March 2015. Her name was Stacy. On November 28, 2015, I received a Facebook message from Stacy. Here is what she wrote:

"Michelle –

I know you don't know me, but I wanted to reach out to you! My name is Stacy. I was recently in a relationship with your ex Paul. Our relationship wasn't all bad -- we definitely had great times that turned into wonderful memories. But when it got bad, it got ugly. I guess, I thought I could change him and believed every word he had spoken. I fell in love with the potential of someone when the potential wasn't there. I was beaten and verbally abused by Paul more than once and it took me one night of getting choked, my head getting smashed through a glass window, and the back of my head getting pounded against the bathroom tile for me to realize this wasn't the person I wanted to become.

First of all, I just wanted to tell you I am so sorry for all that you have gone through. All the pain and confusion you've endured and continually endure. The emotions of still caring, but wanting him to feel as small as he has made you feel, and trying to love someone who has a warped vision of what love is. No one will ever know how it feels until it happens to them (nor do I wish it happens to anyone), but I want you to know I'm sorry you had to experience a sick twisted game of what love was. Love shouldn't be a game of breaking someone down to nothing and making them feel so hopeless and unworthy. I'm not reaching out to you in hopes of a response...I just want to let you know I'm pressing charges so the next girl doesn't have to go through what we went through. And I've realized it's about time I stand up for myself and the others that have to live this nightmare that is on continuous replay.

Lastly, I just want the nightmares to go away, the wounds to heal and for women like you and me to find the inner peace we deserve! He isn't a bad guy, he's just made A LOT of bad decisions, and I don't wish any harm on him whatsoever, but I just hope that he gets the help he needs to deal with the things he hasn't dealt with in his life...and by expresses this to you I hope it gives you a little relief, peace, love and support.

—Stacy"

According to the police report, Paul attacked Stacy and smashed her head through the small glass window in the bathroom of his home. Janelle, the Egyptian woman who worked for Paul from Landmark, came to Stacy's rescue and drove her to her family's home after she had been seen by a local doctor at a nearby hospital.

I felt her beating was partially my fault. I knew the torment she went through and I felt ashamed for letting Paul get away with battering another woman. Through intensive therapy I was forced to realize that I cannot control someone else's actions. I was not responsible for Paul's treatment of Stacy. I was however responsible to assist her in any way possible.

I knew Paul didn't learn from his past, but I was actually surprised and a bit dumbfounded that Paul attacked another woman. Perhaps I was thinking he changed, although he was still emotionally and financially abusing me. Prior to the event concerning Stacy, Paul was negotiating with me to sign a non-disclosure agreement for him to finally payoff our bills. Paul hired his attorneys to draft documents that would inhibit me from speaking about our relationship publicly, offering to pay me for my silence. Paul offered me approximately $175,000 to keep quiet. I am not sure what triggered Paul into creating an NDA, but I have a feeling he thought that I would want to seek justice eventually for his crimes.

I didn't tell Paul I knew what happened to Stacy immediately. I continued playing along with him to see what he would do. Paul wrote me a text on December 8, 2015 that said:

"You will be very happy with what your going to get Michelle... I've had allot to think about and I would like to talk to you tonight about this"

I had a decision to make; I could continue allowing myself and others to be abused by Paul, sign his NDA, and take the money, or I could tell the truth of what happened in our relationship and save lives. If you are reading this book, you can see the route I chose. There was no way I could accept and sign an NDA that prohibited me from telling my story.

This was the actual finality of the relationship. At this point I had endured three years of emotional and physical battering, along with an additional year of psychological manipulation and financial abuse. A total of four years I spent with Paul in my life. My life was completely consumed by this man and now I had to figure everything out on my own. I felt very lost. I was scared of what Paul could do to me and scared of my new life without Paul.

I played along with Paul's games for a month. I asked Paul at the beginning of December 2015, "Are the allegations I read in the newspaper true?" He of course denied them. He said, "Stacy is an alcoholic and a neurotic psychopath." I knew what I had to do. A few days before Christmas, I sent Paul an email explaining my position:

"Did you know I'm an advocate for domestic violence survivors? I have helped 2 women out of domestic violence relationships already and I intend to continue to help more women out of abusive relationships with my story.

I'm worried about you. You are not taking responsibility for the problem you have with abuse- not to Stacy and not completely with me. You are not being truthful about what you did to that young girl.

I am not signing your confidentiality agreement or your non disclosure as it currently reads based on your description. I can't. What I do to help DV survivors, I can't sign your documents. [] My attorney is drafting a proposal for us to settle everything financially.

The DA has contacted me; however, I am unsure if I want to participate in all this. What you've gotten yourself involved in is a big disaster. I'm worried for your well being and I hope you learn and get the help you need. Everything depends on what you do next, but I know I intend to tell the truth and really hope you will also. If you tell the truth, it will be best for you and all involved.

Communication needs to go through my attorney from now on. It is too emotional to talk with you. I can't handle back and forth stress. If we settle our financial issues through our attorneys, I'll be open to communicating with you again. I pray you enjoy time with your family this Christmas and develop a deeper relationship with God. You need Him right now."

Immediately after sending the email, Paul sent me a text:

"Just got your email, I have no idea what you're talking about Michelle, hope you're having a good day."

I told my family and friends the truth of what happened to me and many people encouraged me to continue telling my story. I was full of anxiety. My nightmares got worse. All the dreadful nights Paul and I spent together came rushing back to me. I dreamt that he killed me while strangling me in our bedroom. I dreamt Paul hired an assassin to kill me and I remain fearful when I step into the elevator in my apartment building, thinking as soon as the door opens, someone will be waiting with a Glock 19 on the other side. I won't let my fear overcome me. I fought through my panic-stricken anxiety attacks and decided to move forward by telling the world the awful details of domestic violence.

Chapter Fourteen: Repercussions

January 2016

I am shocked that he hasn't tried to rectify the situation. In the beginning of 2016, life without Paul was difficult. I reminisced driving down the road and watching Paul lip sync "Cruise" by Florida Georgia Line or "Like the Rain" by Clint Black. That's what I missed; the optimistic, cheerful, admirable, wonderfully charismatic man that won my heart. I missed the jokes and laughs while talking about our future together. He was one the biggest dreamers I had ever met; his grandiose visions and desires for life were intoxicating. I look back and think about the great nights, the great days, the amazing times we had together. Outside of his money, outside of his temper and abuse, he was a really great man that I wish would have changed. But he didn't. No matter how hard I prayed or how much I begged, he stayed the same; scorned by his past, abusive to the women in his life, and utterly unfixable.

There were a few occasions where Paul tried to call me and I sent a quick text with no response. One time he called me right before I was interviewed on *TradioV*. I looked at the phone in horror, thinking he could be in town and knew exactly where to find me. I thought he was going to kill me. I almost wanted to back out of the interview, but I stayed strong. Thankfully, I had a friend pray with me right after the phone rang, and the interview happened without a glitch.

Some women can't give up hope that their batterer will change so they stay and/or feel remorse or sorrow for him. I feel pity for Paul. I want him to get the help he needs, but evidence shows that he won't. I spent four years with him and continue to think of the affectionate, sentimental moments we shared. I remember our pillow talks until 3 a.m. and the way he looked at me when he was impressed by something I said or did. We laughed and felt a mutual connection that most people only desire to have. I explain my relationship with Paul as the best and worst relationship of my life.

The first few months of not speaking with Paul were the hardest. One night, I drove down the PCH stopping at a beach in Pacific Palisades where I sat in the sand until 1a.m. crying hysterically, yelling at God, "Why didn't You do something?" The sound of the crashing waves and the smell of salt in the air comforted me.

I found ways to keep myself busy. The times when I had nothing to engross my mind were extremely emotionally draining. I cried so much. I laid in my bed reminiscing about the dreams we dreamt together and the life that we were supposed have. Our perfect and magical fairy tale.

This quote by Steve Maraboli explains exactly how I felt, "I'm not crying because of you; you're not worth it. I'm crying because my delusion of who you were was shattered by the truth of who you are."

I think fondly of the great times, but the catastrophic blowout fights overtake any affectionate feelings I have. Paul never fully embraced the extent of how he physically, emotionally, sexually and financially abused me. He softened the reality of the situation which caused me to question the abuse, by lessoning the severity of it. The emotional torment of Paul's manipulation mixed with the grief of losing my father, and Paul's assault on a new victim, motivated me to seek justice through the legal system. My intention was never to hurt Paul, just to tell the truth and seek damages for what he did to me.

Unfortunately, because of the statute laws in California, I couldn't file criminal charges against him, but I filed civil charges. The DA was already prosecuting him criminally for what he did to Stacy. I hired an attorney and moved forward with a civil suit against him to pursue damages from the abuse I endured for four years.

The process it took to get there was very difficult. I had been seeing Dr. Matt for almost one year and we talked about the possibility of me pressing charges. Dr. Matt said, "If you decide to press charges, you will take your power back from Paul." I wanted closure and I wanted justice.

Of course, I was scared. Paul had financial power and I did not. He owned much of the town he resided in and had many attorneys on retainer. I was always terrified that Paul would find me and kill me. My therapist assured me, "I doubt Paul will take that route because he will be the first person the police are going to suspect."

I fought through my fear and I found a great attorney who helped me maintain my credibility even when Paul attempted to retaliate by using Janelle as a false witness. Paul pressed criminal extortion charges against me and filed a civil extortion and intentional infliction of emotional distress lawsuit with the Los Angeles Police Department. Part of Paul's lawsuit was corroborated by Janelle, the friend who helped Stacy and me out of Paul's abusive grip. I can only imagine what Paul did to Janelle to persuade her to turn her back on us. I was extremely bitter when I found out she was helping Paul. I rationalized her actions because Paul signed her paychecks.

On Feb 23, 2016, Janelle sent me a text message:

"Though you may never trust me again, one day I hope to explain certain things...all I can say atm is that things aren't always what they appear. I love you very much"

Janelle was loyal to me until she was not. I opened up to her about the abuse, but Paul found a way to manipulate her. I was astonished, hurt and confused by her actions, but I got through it. My attorney worked very hard to get the extortion case dropped. We were successful in 2018.

The next few pages represent part of my lawsuit against Paul. Some items and names have been removed:

NATURE OF THE ACTION

1. Plaintiff MICHELLE JEWSBURY had a nearly three (3) year relationship with Defendant []. After suffering repeated instances of outrageous conduct by Defendant, including verbal and physical abuse, assault, battery, and domestic violence, Plaintiff was forced to flee Defendant for her own personal safety. Plaintiff has suffered severe and ongoing long-term trauma and emotional damage and distress as a result of Defendant's abuse and violence. She has suffered significant financial and career damage as a result of Defendant's breach of their partnership agreement. Defendant has failed to honor his promises and commitments to Plaintiff, and Plaintiff now seeks compensation in this lawsuit for Defendant's breaches of contract for his infliction of personal injuries which have caused Plaintiff to suffer extreme, aggravated, and lasting emotional distress.

2. Intentional Tort claims. Defendant, through years of abusive, erratic, and outrageous conduct, including verbal, physical and sexual abuse, caused Plaintiff to suffer severe and lasting emotional distress. Plaintiff is entitled to tort damages, including compensation for severe, aggravated, and lasting emotional distress, as well as compensation for the expense of past and future medical, psychological, and psychiatric treatment and care.

FIRST CAUSE OF ACTION
Domestic Violence (CIV. CODE §1708.6)
(against Defendant WRIGHT)

4-50. (Describe the specific events in this book)
51. Plaintiff incorporates by reference paragraphs 1 through 50 as if fully set forth at length herein.

52. By reason of the above-described conduct, Defendant abused Plaintiff emotionally, mentally, physically and sexually in the course of their relationship, and thus violated Section 1708.6 of the Civil Code.

53. As a result of Defendant's actions and violations of Section 1708.6, Plaintiff has suffered and is continuing to suffer damages, including extreme and severe mental and emotional distress and anguish, loss of sleep, self-esteem, ability to maintain emotional and sexual relationships, complex post-traumatic stress disorder, and acute anxiety. Plaintiff is entitled to general damages, including emotional distress damages, and special damages, including the past and future expense of medical, psychological and psychiatric treatment and care, according to proof at trial.

54. Under California Civil Code Section 1708.6(c), Plaintiff is entitled to an award of attorney's fees and costs.

55. By engaging in the above-described conduct, Defendant is guilty of oppression, fraud, and malice as defined in Section 3294 of the California Civil Code. Accordingly, Plaintiff is entitled to an award of punitive and exemplary damages in an amount sufficient to punish and make an example of Defendant.

SECOND CAUSE OF ACTION
Assault and Battery
(Against Defendant [])

56. Plaintiff hereby incorporates by reference, as set forth in full herein, paragraphs 1 through 55 of this Complaint.

57. Defendant assaulted and battered Plaintiff as described herein.

58. The above-described incidents were in addition to, and part of, a larger pattern of erratic, abusive, aggressive, violent and outrageous behavior and conduct by Defendant directed at Plaintiff as a means of intimidation and control.

59. Defendant's actions were intentional and a product of violent outbursts. Defendant exerted power and control over Plaintiff throughout their entire relationship, to force Plaintiff to act how he wanted. When his words did not change Plaintiff's actions, Defendant resorted to threats and physical violence. Defendant assaulted and battered Plaintiff when her actions did not conform to his wishes, and when she confronted him about his unacceptable behavior. Defendant intended both to scare Plaintiff into acting how he wanted and to harm her as punishment for her disobedience.

60. During the above-described incidents, Plaintiff reasonably believed that Defendant would physically hurt her, based on his years of abusive conduct and need to control her actions.

61. Plaintiff did not consent to any of Defendant's actions.

62. A reasonable person would be offended by Defendant's actions.

63. Defendant's conduct was and is a direct and substantial factor that caused Plaintiff to suffer severe and extreme emotional distress and mental anguish. Defendant's actions have caused Plaintiff to suffer humiliation, embarrassment, and emotional distress. Plaintiff is entitled to general damages, including emotional distress damages, and special damages, including the past and future expense of medical, psychological and psychiatric treatment and care, according to proof at trial.

64. By engaging in the above-described conduct, Defendant is guilty of oppression, fraud, and malice as defined in Section 3294 of the California Civil Code. Accordingly, Plaintiff is entitled to an award of punitive and exemplary damages in an amount sufficient to punish and make an example of Defendant.

THIRD CAUSE OF ACTION
Intentional Infliction of Emotional Distress
(Against Defendant [])

65. Plaintiff hereby incorporates by reference, as set forth in full herein, paragraphs 1 through 64 of this Complaint.

66. Defendant intentionally placed himself in a position of power over the Plaintiff by, among other things, convincing her to quit her employment, give up her career, move from her apartment, cohabitate with Defendant, and rely on Defendant for her food, clothing, shelter and every necessity of life. Once captive, Defendant exploited Plaintiff by subjecting her to emotional, verbal, sexual and physical abuse, as detailed above.

67. Defendant's behavior was outrageous, intentional, and reprehensible. Defendant's manipulation of Plaintiff targeted her deepest weaknesses and fears.

68. As a result of the torment to which Defendant subjected Plaintiff, she has suffered and continues to suffer emotional distress. Plaintiff has continued to suffer from acute panic attacks and has been diagnosed with complex post-traumatic stress disorder, due to Defendant's abuse and outrageous conduct. Plaintiff lives in constant fear that Defendant may disrupt the life she is trying to rebuild for herself.

69. Given Defendant's outrageous and intentional actions in subjecting Plaintiff to severe emotional distress, Plaintiff is entitled to general damages, including emotional distress damages, and special damages, including the past and future expense of medical, psychological and psychiatric treatment and care, according to proof at trial.

70. By engaging in the above-described conduct, Defendant is guilty of oppression, fraud, and malice as defined in Section 3294 of the California Civil Code. Accordingly, Plaintiff is entitled to an award of punitive and exemplary damages in an amount sufficient to punish and make an example of Defendant.

PRAYER

WHEREFORE, Plaintiff demands judgment against all Defendants, jointly and severally, as follows:

1) Compensatory general and special damages in an amount in accordance with proof;
2) Prejudgment interest according to proof;
3) Punitive damages against Defendant;
4) Attorney's fees;
5) Costs of suit necessarily incurred herein; and
6) Such further relief as the Court deems just and proper.

Court proceedings, depositions and negotiations were very painful. The most difficult thing—besides Janelle's fraudulent allegation—was writing over six hundred answers to deposition questions regarding mine and Paul's romantic relationship. I needed to remember specifications about places, dates, what was said, and who was there to witness. I wrote while having big elephant tears streaming down my face.

Paul insisted on going to war with me. He insisted on denying his abuse. He torpedoed missiles in my direction for far too long and I wasn't going to take it any longer. I was not going to back down. I felt incredibly grateful for being able to take my power back.

I debuted my solo play in February 2016 during the Whitefire Solofest. I thought Paul might show up so I hired two security guards to keep me and my audience safe. My goal with the theatrical rendition of *But I Love Him* was to educate the audience about domestic violence. It was a very real look into the life of someone trapped in the cycle of abuse. When the curtain closed, it was so quiet in the theatre you could hear a pin drop. After a few unnerving moments, the audience applauded.

Word got around and women started contacting me in different capacities about domestic violence. I realized I was not alone. Some women heard about me through various interviews and others heard about me from my play. God put me in a position where I was able to encourage women to leave the destructiveness of domestic violence and move into a new world of healthy abundance.

For four years I allowed Paul to control me and abuse me. For four years I gave Paul my heart and soul, condoning his behavior and mistreatment by continually giving him a second, third, and fourth chance. I loved Paul with every fiber of my body even after the beatings, rape and psychological manipulation. I loved Paul because when he was sober he was one of the sweetest people I knew. Looking back, I see how someone could get trapped in a relationship like this. I now can see how I became engrossed in a tumultuous love affair with an abuser.

Author's Final Notes

On November 15, 2018, during a readiness conference for Paul's criminal trial, Paul plead no contest to all five felony charges against him in an open plea—two counts of inflicting corporal injury to a spouse or cohabitant, assault, false imprisonment and dissuading a witness. The actual sentence will be at the judge's discretion after she receives the pre-sentencing probation report, but she stated on record that unless the probation report contains information that has not been previously revealed, she will give Paul...PROBATION.

My attorney called me immediately following the readiness conference. I was in utter shock. Paul assaulted three women in the course of eight years and was going to get away with it.

There are two criminal justice systems in the United States. One is for defendants with wealth or influence who can afford to hire premiere attorneys and who have certain privileges due to the size of their bank accounts. The other system is for everybody else. According to an article written by Eliza Shapiro of *The Daily Beast*, the problem in the courtroom is compounded by high-income husbands who can assemble "legal dream teams," and leave women at the mercy of the system. Paul paid his criminal lawyer almost $500 per hour while Stacy just had the DA helping her. Although Paul is not receiving the sentence he deserves in the criminal case, I will not back down. My civil trial has been continued several times and is scheduled for Spring 2019. I believe my attorney and I will prevail in our civil action.

Oswald Chambers, an early twentieth-century Scottish Baptist and Holiness Movement evangelist, once said, "God brings you to places, among people, and into certain conditions to accomplish a definite purpose..." I believe my purpose is to help men and women involved in domestic violence and sexual assault by telling my story, relaying my experience, and encouraging victims to break free. Society continues to place the responsibility for change on the victims, asking "Why don't you leave?" instead of asking the abuser "Why do you physically, emotionally, and sexually harm the people you love?" People need to understand that in order to stop violence, you have to stop the abuser, not inhibit and blame the victim.

There are many shelters for domestic violence victims, but the demand is greater than the capacity. The first shelter didn't even open until 1964 in the San Gabriel Valley, called Haven House. Beating your wife did not become illegal in the U.S. until 1883 when Maryland finally considered it a crime. Universally, all abusers—whether hitters or drinkers—project blame onto their victims saying it's not their fault, she or he deserved it.

The statistics are startling. Abuse worldwide is a huge epidemic that people have been blindly turning their backs to for many years. I believe one reason is that victims themselves do not admit something is wrong until it is too late. Anyone who goes through abuse needs to speak up. Don't stay silent. The cycle of domestic violence is a destructive and life-threatening problem and can only be eradicated by courageous survivors.

I realize I have permission to rest. If I embrace stillness, I won't get scolded for being lazy, or yelled at for my incompetence. I don't have to try and make everyone happy, I need to focus on myself. Self-love is not selfish. I took a three-month sabbatical the summer of 2016. I traveled to Italy where I was able to spend quality time with God. I also spent time with friends and family in California, Oregon and Idaho.

There is no marketing strategy, social media tactic, bank account, or instructional manual that can heal someone. There is no map to follow for life and no exact way to do things. You have to do the real work of diving deep within yourself to uncover where your sadness lies.

Dr. Matt said, "In order for restoration to take place, you need to feel the uncomfortable and the unconscious." In order to heal, you have to love yourself so that you will be able to love another healthily yet again.

My lifelong goal is to find true happiness, beyond the situational circumstances that life presents, to find peace, and to find true love that lasts forever in Christ. The best thing about all the obstacles I've had, the lessons I've learned, and the pain I've experienced, is that I get to share what I've cultivated with others. To feel is how we learn. To learn is how things change. Through change we can accomplish something of brilliance, majesty, and nobility.

Isaiah 43:18-19 states, *"Forget the former things; do not dwell on the past. See, I am doing a new thing! Now it springs up; do you not perceive it?"*

My lifelong vocation is to help people. God has given me clarity in this. With His help I can use my tragic experience to teach, advise, and aid individuals through domestic abuse.

In July 2017, I founded Unsilenced Voices, a 501(c)3 nonprofit focused on inspiring change in communities around the globe by encouraging victims to break free and survivors to speak up about domestic violence and sexual assault. The mission of Unsilenced Voices is to provide shelter and relief to survivors of domestic abuse and sexual gender-based violence worldwide.

Unsilenced Voices has been operating in Ghana and Sierra Leone where we are working to implement shelters, sensitization programs, legal assistance, vocational training, and medical and counseling to survivors. I've been to both Ghana and Sierra Leone multiple times and we are raising funds to build temporary shelters for victims of domestic abuse and sexual gender based violence in both countries. The organization is currently developing essential partners in the United States to serve the greater Los Angeles area.

I wake up daily and pray Ephesians 6:10-18 for protection. Protection from Paul and protection for all the victims of domestic abuse worldwide.

"Finally, be strong in the Lord and in his mighty power. Put on the full armor of God, so that you can take your stand against the devil's schemes. For our struggle is not against flesh and blood, but against the rulers, against the authorities, against the powers of this dark world and against the spiritual forces of evil in the heavenly realms. Therefore put on the full armor of God, so that when the day of evil comes, you may be able to stand your ground, and after you have done everything, to stand. Stand firm then, with the belt of truth buckled around your waist, with the breastplate of righteousness in place, and with your feet fitted with the readiness that comes from the gospel of peace. In addition to all this, take up the shield of faith, with which you can extinguish all the flaming arrows of the evil one. Take the helmet of salvation and the sword of the Spirit, which is the word of God. And pray in the Spirit on all occasions with all kinds of prayers and requests. With this in mind, be alert and always keep on praying for all the Lord's people."

Resources

Today more than ever, there is help for women who are living with domestic violence. These are some great organizations that may help you break free.

NATIONAL ORGANIZATIONS

American Bar Association Commission on Domestic Violence

740 15th street NW, 9th floor
Washington, DC 20005-1022
(202) 662-1737 or (202) 662-1744
service center to order materials: 1-800-285-2221
Fax: (202) 662-1594
Email: abacdv@abanet.org
www.abanet.org/domviol

Battered Women's Justice Project

1801 Nicollet Ave. S.
Suite 102
Minneapolis, MN 55403
(612) 824-8768
(800) 903-0111 x 1
Fax (612) 824-8965

National Center on Protection Orders and Full Faith & Credit

1901 North Fort Myer Dr., Suite 1011
Arlington, VA 22209
(703) 312-7922
(800) 903-0111 x 2
Fax (703) 312-7966

National Clearinghouse for the Defense of Battered Women

125 South 9th Street, Suite 302
Philadelphia, PA 19017
(215) 351-0010
(800) 903-0111 x 3
Fax (215) 351-0779

National Center on Domestic and Sexual Violence

4612 Shoal Creek Blvd.
Austin, Texas 78756
(800) 799-7233
(800) 656-4673
http://www.ncdsv.org/index.html

Office on Violence Against Women

145 N St., NE, Suite 10W.121
Washington, D.C. 20530
(202)307-6026
Fax (202) 305-2589
Email: ovw.info@usdoj.gov

Domestic Abuse Project (DAP)

204 West Franklin Avenue
Minneapolis, MN 55404
(612) 874-7063
dap@mndap.org

Domestic Abuse Intervention Programs

202 East Superior Street
Duluth, MN 55802
(218) 722-2781
Fax (218) 722-0779

Battered Women's Justice Project

Denise Gamache, Director
dgamache@bwjp.org
(612) 824-8786, ext. 109

Family Services of America

2504 Raeford Road, Suite A Highland Executive Building
Fayetteville, NC 28305
(910) 860-9787
Fax (910) 860-3903
E-mail: info@familiesofusa.com

U.S. National Organizations & Projects
Family Violence Prevention Fund

(415) 252-8900
(800) 595-4889
http://www.endabuse.org/

National Domestic Violence Hotline:

(800) 799-SAFE (7233)
(800) 787-3224 (TTY)

Futures Without Violence

100 Montgomery Street, The Presidio
San Francisco, CA 94129
info@futureswithoutviolence.org
(415) 678-5500
Fax: (415) 529-2930
TTY: (800) 595-4889

Washington, DC Office
1320 19th St. NW, Suite 401
Washington, D.C. 20036
(202) 595-7382
Fax: (202) 299-1292

Boston, MA Office
50 Milk Street, 16th Floor
Boston, MA 02109
(617) 702-2004
Fax: (857) 415-3293

Women Against Abuse

100 South Broad Street, Suite 1341
Philadelphia, PA 19110
(215) 386-1280
http://www.womenagainstabuse.org/index.php
For free legal help from the Women Against Abuse Legal Center,
call (215)686-7082.

National Center for Victims of Crime

2000 M Street NW, Suite 480
Washington, DC 20036
(202) 467-8700
Fax: (202) 467-8701
www.victimsofcrime.org

Women's Law Project

125 S. 9th Street, Suite 300
Philadelphia, PA 19107
(215) 928-9801
info@womenslawproject.org

Women's Law Project Western Pennsylvania

401 Wood Street, Suite 1020
Pittsburgh, PA 15222
(412) 281-2892

NCADV's Main Office

One Broadway, Suite B210
Denver, CO 80203
(303) 839-1852
Fax: (303) 831-9251
Email: mainoffice@ncadv.org

National Council on Child Abuse and Family Violence

1025 Connecticut Avenue NW,Suite 1000
Washington, DC 20036
(202) 429-6695
Email: info@nccafv.org

National Network to End Domestic Violence

1400 16th St NW, Suite 330
Washington, DC 20036
(202) 543-5566
Fax: (202) 543-5626

Love is Respect - the National Dating Abuse Helpline

1-866-331-9474
TTY 1-866-331-8453
Text "loveis" to 22522

Rape, Abuse and Incest National Network

1220 L Street NW, Suite 505
Washington, DC 20005
(202) 544-1034
info@rainn.org
(800) 656-HOPE (4673)

National Council of Juvenile and Family Court Judges

(800) 527-3223
Email fvdinfo@ncjfcj.org

Safe Horizon Crisis Hotlines

Domestic Violence Hotline: (800) 621-HOPE (4673)
Crime Victims Hotline: (866) 689-HELP (4357)
Rape, Sexual Assault & Incest Hotline: (212)227-3000 or (866)689-4357
TDD phone number for all hotlines: (866)604-5350
Email for help (crisis only): help@safehorizon.org

Peace Over Violence

1015 Wilshire Boulevard, Suite 200
Los Angeles, CA 90017
(213) 955-9090

Joyful Heart Foundation

New York
212-475-2026

LGBT Communities and Domestic Violence

6400 Flank Drive, Suite 1300
Harrisburg, Pennsylvania 17112
(800) 537-2238
TTY: (800) 553-2508
Fax: (717)545-9456

STATE COALITION LIST:

Alabama Coalition Against Domestic Violence

P.O. Box 4762
Montgomery, AL 36101
(334) 832-4842
Fax: (334) 832-4803
(800) 650-6522 Hotline
Website: www.acadv.org
Email: info@acadv.org

Alaska Network on Domestic and Sexual Violence

130 Seward Street, Suite 14
Juneau, AK 99801
(907) 586-3650
Fax: (907) 463-4493
Website: www.andvsa.org
Email: andvsa@andvsa.org

Arizona Coalition Against Domestic Violence

2800 N. Central Avenue, Suite 1570
Phoenix, AZ 85004
(602) 279-2900
Fax: (602) 279-2980
(800) 782-6400 Nationwide
Website: www.azcadv.org
Email: acadv@azcadv.org

Arkansas Coalition Against Domestic Violence

1401 West Capitol Avenue, Suite 170
Little Rock, AR 72201
(501) 907-5612
Fax: (501) 907-5618
(800) 269-4668 Nationwide
Website: www.domesticpeace.com
Email: acadv@domesticpeace.com

California Partnership to End Domestic Violence

P.O. Box 1798
Sacramento, CA 95812
(916) 444-7163
Fax: (916) 444-7165
(800) 524-4765 Nationwide
Website: www.cpedv.org
Email: info@cpedv.org

Colorado Coalition Against Domestic Violence

1120 Lincoln Street, Suite 900
Denver, CO 80203
(303) 831-9632
Fax: (303) 832-7067
(888) 778-7091
Website: www.ccadv.org
Email: info@ccadv.org

Connecticut Coalition Against Domestic Violence

912 Silas Deane Highway, Lower Level
Wethersfield, CT 06109
(860) 282-7899
Fax: (860) 282-7892
(888) 774-2900 In-State DV Hotline
Website: www.ctcadv.org
Email: contactus@ctcadv.org

Delaware Coalition Against Domestic Violence

100 West 10th Street, Suite 903
Wilmington, DE 19801
(302) 658-2958
Fax: (302) 658-5049
(800) 701-0456 Statewide
Website: www.dcadv.org
Email: dcadvadmin@dcadv.org

DC Coalition Against Domestic Violence

5 Thomas Circle Northwest
Washington, DC 20005
(202) 299-1181
Fax: (202) 299-1193
Website: www.dccadv.org
Email: info@dccadv.org

Florida Coalition Against Domestic Violence

425 Office Plaza Drive
Tallahassee, FL 32301
(850) 425-2749
Fax: (850) 425-3091
(850) 621-4202 TDD
(800) 500-1119 In State
Website: www.fcadv.org

Georgia Coalition Against Domestic Violence

114 New Street, Suite B
Decatur, GA 30030
(404) 209-0280
Fax: (404) 766-3800
(800) 334-2836 Crisis Line
Website: www.gcadv.org
Email: info@gcadv.org

Hawaii State Coalition Against Domestic Violence

810 Richards Street, Suite 960
Honolulu, HI 96813
(808) 832-9316
Fax: (808) 841-6028
Website: www.hscadv.org
Email: admin@hscadv.org

Idaho Coalition Against Sexual and Domestic Violence

300 E. Mallard Drive, Suite 130
Boise, ID 83706
(208) 384-0419
Fax: (208) 331-0687
(888) 293-6118 Nationwide
Website: www.idvsa.org
Email: info@engagingvoices.org

Illinois Coalition Against Domestic Violence

801 South 11th Street
Springfield, IL 62703
(217) 789-2830
Fax: (217) 789-1939
(217) 242-0376 TTY
Website: www.ilcadv.org
Email: ilcadv@ilcadv.org

Indiana Coalition Against Domestic Violence

1915 West 18th Street, Suite B
Indianapolis, IN 46202
(317) 917-3685
Fax: (317) 917-3695
(800) 332-7385 In State
Website: www.icadvinc.org
Email: icadv@icadvinc.org

Iowa Coalition Against Domestic Violence

3030 Merle Hay Road
Des Moines, IA 50312
(515) 244-8028
Fax: (515) 244-7417
(800) 942-0333 In State Hotline
Website: www.icadv.org
Email: icadv@icadv.org

Kansas Coalition Against Sexual and Domestic Violence

634 Southwest Harrison Street
Topeka, KS 66603
(785) 232-9784
Fax: (785) 266-1874
Website: www.kcsdv.org
Email: coalition@kcsdv.org

Kentucky Domestic Violence Association

111 Darby Shire Circle
Frankfort, KY 40601
(502) 209-5382
Fax: (502) 226-5382
Website: www.kdva.org
Email: info@kdva.org

Louisiana Coalition Against Domestic Violence

P.O. Box 77308
Baton Rouge, LA 70879
(225) 752-1296
Fax: (225) 751-8927
Website: www.lcadv.org
Email: info@lcadv.org

Maine Coalition To End Domestic Violence

One Weston Court, Box #2
Augusta, ME 04330
(207) 430-8334
Fax: (207) 430-8348
Website: www.mcedv.org
Email: info@MCADV.org

Maryland Network Against Domestic Violence

4601 Presidents Drive, Suite 370
Lanham, MD 20706
(301) 352-4574
Fax: (301) 809-0422
(800) 634-3577 Nationwide
Website: www.mnadv.org
Email: info@mnadv.org

Jane Doe, Inc./Massachusetts Coalition Against Sexual Assault and Domestic Violence

14 Beacon Street, Suite 507
Boston, MA 02108
(617) 248-0922
Fax: (617) 248-0902
(617) 263-2200 TTY/TDD
Website: www.janedoe.org
Email: info@janedoe.org

Michigan Coalition Against Domestic and Sexual Violence

3893 Okemos Road, Suite B-2
Okemos, MI 48864
(517) 347-7000 Phone/TTY
Fax: (517) 248-0902
Website: www.mcedsv.org
Email: general@mcedsv.org

Minnesota Coalition For Battered Women

60 E. Plato Blvd., Suite 130
St. Paul, MN 55107
(651) 646-6177
Fax: (651) 646-1527
(651) 646-0994 Crisis Line
(800) 289-6177 Nationwide
Website: www.mcbw.org
Email: mcbw@mcbw.org

Mississippi Coalition Against Domestic Violence

P.O. Box 4703
Jackson, MS 39296
(601) 981-9196
Fax: (601) 981-2501
(800) 898-3234
Website: www.mcadv.org
Email: support@mcadv.org

Missouri Coalition Against Domestic and Sexual Violence

217 Oscar Drive, Suite A
Jefferson City, MO 65101
(573) 634-4161
Fax: (573) 636-3728
Website: www.mocadsv.org
Email: mocadsv@mocadsv.org

Montana Coalition Against Domestic & Sexual Violence

P.O. Box 818
Helena, MT 59624
(406) 443-7794
Fax: (406) 443-7818
(888) 404-7794 Nationwide
Website: www.mcadsv.com
Email: mtcoalition@mcadsv.com

Nebraska Domestic Violence Sexual Assault Coalition

245 S. 84th Street, Suite 200
Lincoln, NE 68510
(402) 476-6256
Fax: (402) 476-6806
(800) 876-6238 In State Hotline
(877) 215-0167 Spanish Hotline
Website: www.ndvsac.org
Email: help@ndvsac.org

Nevada Network Against Domestic Violence

250 South Rock BLVD., Suite 116
Reno, NV 89502
(775) 828-1115
Fax: (775) 828-9911
Website: www.nnadv.org
Email: info@nnadv.org

New Hampshire Coalition Against Domestic and Sexual Violence

P.O. Box 353
Concord, NH 03302
(603) 224-8893
Fax: (603) 228-6096
(866) 644-3574 In State
Website: www.nhcadsv.org
Email: info@nhcadsv.org

New Jersey Coalition for Battered Women

1670 Whitehorse Hamilton Square Road
Trenton, NJ 08690
(609) 584-8107
Fax: (609) 584-9750
(800) 572-7233 In State
Website: www.njcbw.org
Email: info@njcbw.org

New Mexico Coalition Against Domestic Violence

1210 Luisa Street, Suite 7
Santa Fe, NM 87505
(505) 246-9240
Fax: (505) 246-9434
(800) 773-3645 In State
Website: www.nmcadv.org
Email: info@nmcadv.org

New York State Coalition Against Domestic Violence

119 Washington Avenue, 3rd Floor
Albany, NY 12054
(518) 482-5464
Fax: (518) 482-3807
(800) 942-5465 English-In State
(800) 942-6908 Spanish-In State
Website: www.nyscadv.org
Email: nyscadv@nyscadv.org

North Carolina Coalition Against Domestic Violence

3710 University Drive, Suite 140
Durham, NC 27707
(919) 956-9124
Fax: (919) 682-1449
(888) 997-9124
Website: www.nccadv.org

North Dakota Council on Abused Women's Services

525 N. 4th Street
Bismarck, ND 5850
(701) 255-6240
Fax: (701) 255-1904
(888) 255-6240 Nationwide
Website: www.ndcaws.org
Email: contact@cawsnorthdakota.org

Action Ohio Coalition For Battered Women

5900 Roche Drive, Suite 445
Columbus, OH 43229
(614) 825-0551
Fax: (614) 825-0673
(888) 622-9315 In State
Website: www.actionohio.org
Email: actionohio@wowway.biz

Ohio Domestic Violence Network

4807 Evanswood Drive, Suite 201
Columbus, OH 43229
(614) 781-9651
Fax: (614) 781-9652
(614) 781-9654 TTY
(800) 934-9840
Website: www.odvn.org
Email: info@odvn.org

Oklahoma Coalition Against Domestic Violence and Sexual Assault

3815 North Santa Fe Avenue, Suite 124
Oklahoma City, OK 73118
(405) 524-0700
Fax: (405) 524-0711
Website: www.ocadvsa.org
Email: prevention@ocadvsa.org

Oregon Coalition Against Domestic and Sexual Violence

1737 NE Alberta Street, Suite 205
Portland, OR 97211
(503) 230-1951
Fax: (503) 230-1973
(877) 230-1951
Website: www.ocadsv.com
Email: adminasst@ocadsv.com

Pennsylvania Coalition Against Domestic Violence

3605 Vartan Way, Suite 101
Harrisburg, PA 17110
(717) 545-6400
Fax: (717) 545-9456
(800) 932-4632 Nationwide
Website: www.pcadv.org

The Office of Women Advocates

Box 11382
Fernandez Juancus Station
Santurce, PR 00910
(787) 721-7676
Fax: (787) 725-9248

Rhode Island Coalition Against Domestic Violence

422 Post Road, Suite 102
Warwick, RI 02888
(401) 467-9940
Fax: (401) 467-9943
(800) 494-8100 In State
Website: www.ricadv.org
Email: ricadv@ricadv.org

South Carolina Coalition Against Domestic Violence and Sexual Assault

P.O. Box 7776
Columbia, SC 29202
(803) 256-2900
Fax: (803) 256-1030
(800) 260-9293 Nationwide
Website: www.sccadvasa.org

South Dakota Coalition Against Domestic Violence & Sexual Assault

P.O. Box 141
Pierre, SD 57501
(605) 945-0869
Fax: (605) 945-0870
(800) 572-9196 Nationwide
Website: www.sdcedsv.org
Email: donnalyn@sdcadvsa.org

Tennessee Coalition Against Domestic and Sexual Violence

2 International Plaza Drive, Suite 425
Nashville, TN 37217
(615) 386-9406
Fax: (615) 383-2967
(800) 289-9018 In State
Website: www.tncoalition.org
Email: tcadsv@tcadsv.org

Texas Council On Family Violence

P.O. Box 163865
Austin, TX 78716
(512) 794-1133
Fax: (512) 794-1199
Website: www.tcfv.org

Utah Domestic Violence Council

205 North 400 West
Salt Lake City, UT 84103
(801) 521-5544
Fax: (801) 521-5548
Website: www.udvc.org

Vermont Network Against Domestic Violence and Sexual Assault

P.O. Box 405
Montpelier, VT 05601
(802) 223-1302
Fax: (802) 223-6943
(802) 223-1115 TTY
Website: www.vtnetwork.org
Email: vtnetwork@vtnetwork.org

Women's Coalition of St. Croix

P.O. Box 222734
Christiansted
St. Croix, VI 00822
(340) 773-9272
Fax: (340) 773-9062
Website: www.wcstx.com
Email: info@wcstx.org

Virginia Sexual & Domestic Violence Action Alliance

5008 Monument Avenue, Suite A
Richmond, VA 23230
Office: 804.377.0335
Fax: 804.377.0339
Website: www.vsdvalliance.org
E-mail: info@vsdvalliance.org

Washington State Coalition Against Domestic Violence

Olympia:
711 Capitol Way, Suite 702
Olympia, WA 98501
(360) 586-1022
Fax: (360) 586-1024
(360) 586-1029 TTY

Seattle:
1402 Third Avenue, Suite 406
Seattle, WA 98101
(206) 389-2515 Fax: (206) 389-2520
(800) 886-2880 In State
(206) 389-2900 TTY
Website: www.wscadv2.org
Email: wscadv@wscadv.org

Washington State Native American Coalition Against Domestic and Sexual Assault

P.O. Box 13260
Olympia, WA 98508
(360) 352-3120
Fax: (360) 357-3858
(888) 352-3120
Website: www.womenspirit.net

West Virginia Coalition Against Domestic Violence

5004 Elk River Road South
Elkview, WV 25071
(304) 965-3552
Fax: (304) 965-3572
Website: www.wvcadv.org
Email: website@wvcadv.org

Wisconsin Coalition Against Domestic Violence

1245 East Washington Avenue, Suite 150
Madison, WI 53703
(608) 255-0539
Fax: (608) 255-3560
Website: www.wcadv.org
Email: wcadv@wcadv.org

Wyoming Coalition Against Domestic Violence and Sexual Assault

P.O. Box 236
710 Garfield Street, Suite 218
Laramie, WY 82073
(307) 755-5481
Fax: (307) 755-5482
(800) 990-3877 Nationwide
Website: www.wyomingdvsa.org
Email: info@wyomingdvsa.org

INTERNATIONAL ORGANIZATIONS:

UN Women

220 East 42nd Street
New York, NY 10017
(646) 781-4400
www.unwomen.org

Global Fund for Women

222 Sutter Street, Suite 500
San Francisco, CA 94108, USA
(415) 248-4800

International Rescue Committee

122 East 42nd Street
New York, NY 10168, USA
(212) 551-3000

Women's Refugee Commission

122 East 42nd Street
New York, NY 10168 , USA
(212) 551-3115

Women Against Violence Europe

Bacherplatz 10 / 4, 1050
Vienna, Austria
+43-(0)1-5482720

Women For Women International
4455 Connecticut Ave NW, Suite 200
Washington, DC 20008, USA
(202) 737-7705

Jewish Women International

1129 20th Street NW, Suite 801
Washington, DC, 20036
United States
1-800-343-2823

World Health Organization

WHO Headquarters in Geneva
Avenue Appia 20
1202 Geneva
Telephone: +41-22-7912111

MEN'S PROGRAMS:

AMEND (Abusive Men Exploring New Directions)

2727 Bryant St. # 350
Denver, Colorado 80211, United States
(303) 832-6363
Website: http://www.amendinc.org

Batterer's Anonymous Program
Stop Violence Against Women

330 Second Avenue South, Suite 800
Minneapolis, MN 55401, USA
(612) 341-3302
Fax: (612) 341-2971
Email: hrights@advrights.org

Emerge: Counseling and Education to stop Domestic Violence Because Wanting to Stop is NOT Enough

2464 Massachusetts Avenue, Suite 101
Cambridge, MA 02140
(617) 547-9879
Fax: 617-547-0904
info@emergedv.com

Men Overcoming Violence

1385 Mission St,
San Francisco, CA 94103
(415) 626-6704
http://menovercomingviolence.org/

RAVEN
Organization for changing men

1914 Olive St.
St. Louis, MO 63103
(314)289.8000

Bibliography

Anderson, K. & DaGradi, D. (Producer), Geronimi, C. (Director). (1959) *Sleeping Beauty* [Motion Picture]. United States: Buena Vista Film Distribution Company.

The Andy Warhol Foundation for the Visual Arts (2017) *WARHOL ON LOVE: 12 QUOTES FROM THE KING OF POP ART*. Retrieved from http://warhol.christies.com/warhol-on-love-12-quotes-from-the-king-of-pop-art/.

The Daily Beast (2013) *Domestic Violence Among the Wealthy Hides Behind 'Veil of Silence'*. Retrieved from https://www.thedailybeast.com/domestic-violence-among-the-wealthy-hides-behind-veil-of-silence.

Berry J.D, Dawn Bradley (2005) *The Domestic Violence Sourcebook Third Edition*. (Forward, Susan) (any behavior that is interceded to control and subjugate another human being through the use of fear, humiliation and verbal or physical assaults... it is the systematic persecution of one partner by another) Los Angeles: Lovell House Publishing.

Berry J.D, Dawn Bradley (2005) *The Domestic Violence Sourcebook Third Edition*. Los Angeles: Lovell House Publishing.

Berry J.D, Dawn Bradley (2005) *The Domestic Violence Sourcebook Third Edition*. (Jacobson, Dr. Neil & Gottman, John M.) (she is going insane by systematically denying her experience of reality and contradicting her experiences- especially of his abuse-until she begins to doubt her own sanity. This, they believe, may be the ultimate form of abuse- to gain control of the victims mind.) Los Angeles: Lovell House Publishing.

Berry J.D, Dawn Bradley (2005) *The Domestic Violence Sourcebook Third Edition*. (Steven Stosny) Los Angeles: Lovell House Publishing.

Berry J.D, Dawn Bradley (2005) *The Domestic Violence Sourcebook Third Edition*. (Walker, Lenore) (Battering is not a "fight" that involves two people. Often, violence will be triggered by something utterly insignificant) Los Angeles: Lovell House Publishing.

Criminal Justice Statistics Center Report Series (1999) Report on Arrests for Domestic Violence in California, 1998. Retrieved from https://oag.ca.gov/sites/all/files/agweb/pdfs/cjsc/publications/misc/dv98.pdf.

Domestic Abuse Intervention Project of Duluth, Minnesota (2016) *Behaviors of Abusive Men*. Retrieved from https://www.theduluthmodel.org/.

"Domestic Violence." Merriam-Webster.com. Merriam-Webster, n.d. Web. 6 May 2018.

Domestic Violence and Sexual Assault Guide (2009) *Cycle of Domestic Violence*. p.10. Retrieved from http://www.courts.ca.gov/documents/Lyndas_Training_Guide.pdf.

Good Reads (2017) *Quotable Quote*. Retrieved from https://www.goodreads.com/quotes/751146-i-m-not-crying-because-of-you-you-re-not-worth-it.

Graph of The Cycle of Domestic Violence: Adapted from Lenore Walker, The Battered Woman, Harper and Row, 1979

Haugen, David M. (2000) *Domestic Violence: Opposing Viewpoints*. Michigan: Greenhaven Press, Inc.

Haugen, David M. (2000) *Domestic Violence: Opposing Viewpoints*. 34, 38 (Tamara L. Roleff ed., 2000) (according to the Department of Justice, women are victims of domestic violence eleven times more often than men) Michigan: Greenhaven Press, Inc.

Haugen, David M. (2000) *Domestic Violence: Opposing Viewpoints*. (Each year an estimated two to four million American women will be physically and/or sexually abused by their male partners. An estimated 30 percent to 66 percent of these women will call the police for help). Michigan: Greenhaven Press, Inc.

Haugen, David M. (2000) *Domestic Violence: Opposing Viewpoints*. (Studies have shown that though domestic violence is universal, it is more prevalent in substance abusers. F. Hilberman and M. Munson found that 93 percent of the persons causing violence on their wives were alcoholics. Marvin E. Wolfgang reported that in his study, 67 percent of husbands who beat their wives were alcoholics). Michigan: Greenhaven Press, Inc.

Landmark (2017) *Redefine What's Possible.* Retrieved from http://www.landmarkworldwide.com/.

Morgan-Steiner, Leslie (2009) *Crazy Love.* New York: St. Martin's Press.

Nakazawa, Donna Jackson (2015) *Childhood Disrupted : How Your Biography Becomes Your Biology, and How You Can Heal.* New York: Atria Books.

The National Coalition Against Domestic Violence (2017) *Statistics*. Retrieved from https://ncadv.org/statistics.

The National Domestic Violence Hotline (2018) *50 Obstacles to Leaving*. Retrieved from https://www.thehotline.org/2013/06/10/50-obstacles-to-leaving-1-10.

National Network to End Domestic Violence (2017) *About Financial Abuse*. Retrieved from https://nnedv.org/content/about-financial-abuse/.

NNEDV Women's Law.Org (2019) *Sexual Assault/Rape*. Retrieved from https://www.womenslaw.org/about-abuse/forms-abuse/sexual-abuse-and-exploitation/sexual-assault-rape/all.

The United States Department of Justice (2017) *Domestic Violence*. Retrieved from https://www.justice.gov/ovw/domestic-violence#dv.

Women's Resource Center (2017) *Domestic Violence and Abuse*. Retrieved from http://www.womensresourcecenter.org/domestic-violence-abuse.

Acknowledgements

I would have not had the courage or strength to write this book if my friends and family had not been there for me. I appreciate all the people mentioned in this book with special thanks to Mom, Dad, Josh, Jorine, Douglas, Brittany, Chelsea, Rachel, Ralph, Alan, Jessica, and Dan.

About the Author

Michelle Jewsbury is an international philanthropist and humanitarian that has traveled the world as an advocate for the less fortunate. In May 2014, she took her first humanitarian trip to Guatemala where she helped an orphanage on the Rio Dulce. Her next mission trip took her to Kenya, Africa with Kizimani, a nonprofit that focuses on bringing hope and sustainable change to impoverished communities. In 2015, she embarked in a career as Vice President for Young Vision Africa, a nonprofit organization that encourages young leaders in Sierra Leone to make lasting changes in their country. Also in 2015, Michelle joined a team of people in Hyderabad, India where she worked with Back2Back at one of their orphanages. Michelle left her position with Young Vision Africa in August 2016 to focus her efforts on ending domestic violence.

In the entertainment industry, Michelle has worked in casting, as an agent, producer, and actress in television, film, and on the stage. Michelle wrote, produced, and performed a critically acclaimed play about her experience with the same title. The play debuted at the largest Solo Festival on the West Coast, The Whitefire Solofest, with a nearly sold out performance in February 2016. The show, also staged in the 2016 Hollywood Fringe Festival, received multiple reviews and commendations.

Michelle has had numerous appearances on talk shows, speaking engagements, and workshops and has led multiple seminars on the harsh reality of violence against women. Michelle's hope is that through her bravery and boldness she will inspire others to participate in ending domestic violence and sexual assault.

Made in the USA
Monee, IL
12 June 2021